The Art of Mastering Sales Management

Thomas A. Cook

CRC Press
Taylor & Francis Group
Boca Raton   London   New York

CRC Press is an imprint of the
Taylor & Francis Group, an **Informa** business

CRC Press
Taylor & Francis Group
6000 Broken Sound Parkway NW, Suite 300
Boca Raton, FL 33487-2742

© 2010 by Taylor and Francis Group, LLC
CRC Press is an imprint of Taylor & Francis Group, an Informa business

Printed in the United States of America on acid-free paper
10 9 8 7 6 5 4 3 2

International Standard Book Number: 978-1-4200-9075-8 (Hardback)

Library of Congress Cataloging-in-Publication Data

Cook, Thomas A., 1953-
 The art of mastering sales management / Thomas A. Cook.
  p. cm.
 Includes bibliographical references and index.
 ISBN 978-1-4200-9075-8
 1. Sales management. I. Title.

HF5438.4.C666 2010
658.8'1--dc22   2009022076

Visit the Taylor & Francis Web site at
http://www.taylorandfrancis.com

and the CRC Press Web site at
http://www.crcpress.com

Dedicated to all the American soldiers who fight everyday to preserve the ideals
and beliefs of this nation and particularly to those who shed blood...
Irrespective of politics, sentiments, or personal positions.
God Bless Them All.
And let us be grateful for all we have.

Contents

Introduction

Corporations have changed their marketing and selling processes to accommodate a new world order following the stock market decline in 1999/2000 and the events of September 11, 2001.

Globalization, customer service, leadership, lower margins, and longer and harder working hours have become the norm.

This book will dissect the current-events issues that have changed the art of selling and offer "hands-on" strategies, techniques, and easy execution-able tips to higher-end sales personnel and those who manage them.

The author is a seasoned salesman, marketing tycoon, and sales manager with numerous failures and successes to share with the reader. The experience spans six continents, 80 countries, and 12 different business platforms and has spanned 35 years.

The focus of the book is on setting sales strategy, providing exemplary leadership, and developing skill sets to successfully manage sales personnel, team initiatives, and corporate growth plans.

The book becomes a very useful desk reference manual for sales managers in all the aspects of managing, handling, and dealing with sales personnel issues. From the very best of circumstances to the very worse—it is all covered in detail.

The author shows how to be creative in problem solving and offers a very direct, no nonsense guide for getting the best from your sales people and keeping them as long-term contributing and motivated employees.

The book concludes in setting up a daily regimen for the sales manager to keep him or her on track on his or her responsibilities and a clear and concise direction for success.

THOUGHTS TO SELL BY...

Daring ideas are like chessmen moved forward; they may be beaten, but they may start a winning game.

Johann Wolfgang von Goethe

Acknowledgments

The American Management Association
Neil Lenok
Annette Homan
Binder Riha Associates
World Trade Institute
The World Academy
American River International

Chapter 1

The Importance of Leadership in Sales Management

This chapter looks at the differences between management and leadership and outlines the necessary steps to accomplish both.

Overview

- What are leadership and management?
- Can they be learned, enhanced, and mastered?
- Are they innate? Are leaders born, made, or matured?

These questions are critical in succeeding in sales and sales management!

Most business philosophies identify management as the role of supervising employees, keeping organized, communicating effectively, and handling the various tasks to deliver the results dictated by "senior management and the company."

Leadership is a more complex concept. I believe it is a quality that allows a person to successfully lead a group of people into battle, effect change, modify behavior, and raise people's abilities to greater heights.

Are all managers leaders? Are all leaders managers? Neither is necessarily true.

Who do we know in public life in the last 75 years who were great leaders? Winston Churchill, Franklin Roosevelt, Ronald Reagan, John Kennedy, to name a few. Who were great managers? Jimmy Carter, Joe Torre, Alan Greenspan, Colin Powell, to name a few.

Why do we see some as great managers versus others as great leaders? The difference is that those who have leadership attached to their persona were able to inspire, motivate, and cause change in big ways. Those who were managers were successful because they appeared organized, mature, collected, centered, and could approach their responsibilities well.

Some characteristics of managers and leaders are similar. But the main division comes in the ability to effect change. The leader has a following. He or she gets people to believe and motivates them to modify behavior and produce results. The manager manages tasks, activities, and responsibilities, hopefully well.

The military—the Department of Defense—spends millions of dollars to determine what makes good managers and leaders. It is always a controversial subject as to whether leaders can be made and whether managers can be made.

This author has come to the following conclusions:

Leadership is innate. It can be enhanced, and it can be further developed through experience and learning curves, but one has it from birth and develops it as he or she matures.

Certain management qualities are innate, but most can be learned through experience.

There are fewer leaders than managers, making good leaders harder to find. That is why there are fewer CEOs than vice presidents and fewer business entrepreneurs than there are managers.

The expression, "Cream rises to the top," is both true and false. It is true that leaders rise to the occasion. But it is false in the sense that all managers will rise to senior levels of business. Those who possess both leadership and management qualities—in balance—will have the best opportunities for success in running businesses and creating the most dynamic sales organizations.

I just mentioned the word "balance." What I mean is that leadership and management skill sets are critical to a person's success, but only when they are balanced with each other.

We all know people who have leadership qualities but are overwhelming, sometimes even to the point of being arrogant or obnoxious. We all know good managers who are too anal, too picayune, or even too organized. We end up having disdain for these individuals, no matter how successful they are. But those individuals who have leadership and management character traits and skill sets that combine the best of both are better in leading personnel in any organization. Excessiveness in almost anything will eventually fail.

Sales managers who work on their leadership and management skills in a more harmonic and balanced approach will find it easier to adapt to and work with others. This balance will lead to more productive activities and greater levels of success.

Sales managers have to effect change in people. They have to encourage. They have to promote, advocate, and endorse. They have to manage initiatives. They have to organize individuals into teams. They have to coach and mentor.

Their best shot at getting that all done consistently and successfully is to balance out the necessary capabilities as a good leader and manager. They will earn more respect and find it easier to achieve results from the people who work for them.

How can we do this? In three steps:

1. Learn what you have. Identify your leadership skills and talents. Understand your management prowess. Identify your strengths and weaknesses. This requires a lot of introspective insight and the possibility of outside testing and personality-revealing options. This will depend on how honest you are with yourself and your ability "to see the forest through the trees" in your own self-analysis.
2. Seek assistance from outside agencies. Seminars, consultants, reading, Internet, and sales management associations are but a few of the options here. Business schools such as the American Management Association, the World Academy, Dale Carnegie Training, and IOMA are but a few of the very professional and competent educational options that you can turn to.

   www.amanet.org
   www.theworldacademy.com
   www.dalecarnegie.com
   www.ioma.com

3. Benchmark your initiatives. Continually work at seeing how you are progressing. Set aggressive but achievable goals, and have several independent persons advise you on where you are at and what else needs to be done.

Many sales managers utilize professional mentors or consultants to help them with this area of responsibility of receiving independent advice and status.

Mentoring, Coaching, Teaching, Supervising, Managing, and Leading

Mentoring, coaching, teaching, supervising, managing, and leading are all very interconnected and, by some definitions and practice, can all be one in the same. They all point a person in the right direction and enable him or her to get there.

They all show someone how to do something. They all establish an action for someone to take. They all pass information and demonstrate its value.

Mentoring

The dictionary definition of *mentor* is "a close, trusted, experienced counselor or guide." In business, we think of a mentor as a person we look up to and who shows us the way by example.

To have the nameplate "Mentor" is typically a thing to be proud of and feel good about. It is generally all positive. To have a mentor in life and in business creates immediate and significant advantage to a person, and in sales it can mean the difference between success and failure in certain trades and industries.

Coaching

The dictionary definition of a *coach* is "one who instructs or trains." We think mostly of coaches relative to athletics and sports (Figure 1.1). We envision the older and larger former champion sharing his or her talent and experience to bring out the best in us.

We envision someone championing us on to victory; picking us up when we are down and motivating us to try harder; sharing with us his or her strengths and making them work for us.

This is all and every part of what coaches do for us in business and in sales management. And they are often inspiring.

Teaching

The dictionary defines a *teacher* as "one who shows, guides, and instructs." We think of teachers as individuals who talk to us about specific subjects and the necessary skill sets we need to grow and succeed.

Teaching is generally accomplished in a formal and structured environment.

As sales managers, we need to teach some very specific skill sets and capabilities (Figure 1.2).

Supervising

The dictionary tells us that *supervising* involves direction and oversight. Sales managers must direct and oversee the sales personnel that report to them.

We envision supervisors wearing visors and shirt cuffs, standing over us and annunciating orders and shouting commands.

As managers, we do have to exercise supervisory actions, which can be micromanaging our staff on a transactional or specific subject-matter basis. "Supervision"

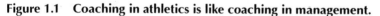

Figure 1.1   Coaching in athletics is like coaching in management.

is usually narrower in scope then overall "management," and in many organizations it is a step just before being elevated to manager.

Managing

A manager is defined as one who trains, handles, directs, plans, organizes, coordinates, etc. Many also expand this definition to include the additional responsibility of obtaining certain "results."

Managing is clearly a larger and more pronounced theater of responsibility than supervising. It greatly increases and enhances the overall scope that the "supervisor" is now held accountable for. Fostering growth is part of management (Figure 1.3).

Management at this level is involved with making money and profits for the company. In sales management, the central theme is an array of skill sets and responsibilities to meet the goals of the company in account retention, new business development, and profitability.

Figure 1.2 Teaching computer skill sets.

Leading

Leadership is a much harder trait to understand. The dictionary tells us that it is "to cause to go with oneself, to convey and to guide, to provide direction."

The author's definition of leadership, particularly in business and in sales, is for an individual to create a persona that changes behavior in a direction that causes goals, plans, and deliverables to be met.

Of all the skills—mentoring, coaching, teaching, supervising, managing, and leading—leading is the most difficult to achieve. In this book, we will discuss this subject in greater detail.

Leadership has certain innate qualities that give a person this capability. It is the hardest to achieve because it is more difficult not only to learn, but to put to successful practice. One could be a good supervisor, manager, or teacher and not necessarily be a good leader.

Leadership makes change happen, and change is one of the hardest human qualities to come by. Good leaders can enhance and grow established skill sets in any area and hone their leadership qualities with training, experience, and continual information flow.

Information flow through informal and formal training, seminar participation, Web-site utilization, and reading of periodicals is your best option. Spending anywhere from 3% to as much as 10% of your time in this information flow and learning-process development is a key to leadership growth and promotion.

THOUGHTS TO SELL BY...

Live in the sunshine, swim the sea, drink the wild air.

Ralph Waldo Emerson

Chapter 2

Making Sure the Goals of Corporate Conform to the Sales and Marketing Initiatives

Most corporations set goals. These goals typically include growth, profit, branding, and customer retention. These all engage the responsibility of sales staff and sales management influence and control.

Growth

Most companies anticipate growth from year to year. Growth in sales, new business, new products, and in the count of sales staff are general areas of anticipated growth. The sales manager who inherits these goals will always be better off when he or she participates in the goal-setting process. In some companies the sales manager will easily sit in a position of influencing goal setting. This is a good situation. Others may have to negotiate their way into this arena. Regardless, the more the sales manager can influence growth goals, the more likely it is that the net result will be more realistic and doable goals.

In my consulting practice on sales management, when companies see a drop in growth or poor performance, a major cause of that circumstance is directly attributed to the "disconnect" between those who set goals and those who have to execute those goals. The role of the sales manager is to align the desires and wishes of senior management with the realities, limitations, and opportunities that are likely to be accomplished by the sales staff. Often the banter and communications that take place between senior management and sales management will allow certain support and infrastructure changes to be accomplished to assist in goal setting. The following is an example of this:

A company selling landscaping equipment began to lose market share in its Midwest region, which historically had been a very successful business area. In 2007 it pushed its sales force into new and very high-growth business goals. The goals were set with no dialogue between senior management and sales management. By the end of the year, sales fell very short of goals. No one was happy, both in senior management and in sales management. With the poor growth, the sales staff was very unhappy and started to leave the company and go to competitors as they began to lose personal revenue when sales did not pick up.

In another scenario, the sales manager was able to influence senior management in the goal-setting process. The sales manager advised the president of the company that a significant reason for the loss in sales was directly due to their inability to handle financing of machinery and equipment through their own leasing company, as some of their competitors did. The sales manager further advised that, if this problem were not fixed, they would never be able to grow sales and would probably continue to lose existing accounts and market share. The sales manager said that in order for sales to meet the aggressive growth plans, machinery financing would be a critical tool. As a result of this dialogue, the president of the company agreed with the rationale and took steps to establish a relationship with an exclusive local bank to offer equipment financing at very competitive terms. This resulted in a stabilization of the problem in three months and new sales growth by six months and record sales by the end of the year.

Sales managers who are given the privilege of influencing growth can utilize the following matrix of goals, strategies, and tactics to assist in their effort.

Goals, Strategies, and Tactics

- We who work in sales management will always be in a position to develop goals.
- We sales managers will then have to come up with strategies on how to deliver these goals.
- We will then have to decide the tactics that will lead to successful implementation of the strategies that will help us meet our goals.

The three concepts are connected at the hip. Technically, you cannot have one without the other. And one will be totally dependent on the other in order to be successful. Let us view an example:

Roger, director of sales of an oil pipeline supply company in Houston, Texas, has agreed to go along with senior management's directive for the upcoming year—to increase account retention to 97%, up 4% from this past year, and to increase new account sales by 15%, up 5% from this past year. These percentage increases are the goals.

Bob now must come up with strategies to accomplish these goals. He develops several specific strategies for each deliverable.

Deliverable: Account Retention / 4% increase
Strategies for Account Retention:

1. Offer renewal discounts to existing clients with early renewal commitments.
2. Bring out an additional value-added service, which IT has been working on the past 6 months.
3. Increase renewal incentives for all sales personnel.

Tactics for Account Retention:

1. Have a meeting with all sales personnel in a team setting to announce the new goals and strategies and the role they will all play in the development of the new deliverables for the upcoming year. At this point you will outline the new incentives, as a motivation technique.
2. You will set individual sales personnel meetings within 2 days of the team session to outline individual goals and requirements.
3. A sales piece will be developed in conjunction with marketing and IT and sent out to all existing accounts by the end of the month announcing the new value-added IT service, with the point of impressing and motivating clients to renew with you.
4. A second communication will be hand-delivered by all sales personnel within two weeks of the first communication—announcing the incentives for early-renewal commitments. Sales personnel will attempt to close these renewals or at least obtain commitments.
5. Once the deliverables are happening, a celebration dinner will occur with you, your boss, and all sales personnel, with incentive checks being handed out for all the successful renewals. This demonstrates appreciation and will be highly motivating to keep up all the efforts of early commitments and increased renewal retention.

Deliverable: New Account Sales / 5% increase
Strategies for New Account Sales:

1. Open up two new regions.
2. Lower price points on larger accounts by 3%.
3. Offer overrides, bonuses, and commission incentives to sales personnel with new business growth that exceeds individual goals.

Tactics for New Account Sales:

1. Hire two additional sales personnel, seasoned in the two new regions you are looking to develop, that control books of business and that have a client following.
2. Meet with key operations managers to see where price breaks can be given without sacrificing net gains. Agree to price breaks.
3. Meet with all sales personnel in a combined business and social setting to "set up" the new sales tactics and explain how they will all benefit from the new business initiatives and commission overrides.
4. Agree to an action plan specifying who will do what and by when and then execute.

Follow-up

In both cases you need to meet on a regular basis following the execution to see if the strategies or the tactics need to be tweaked or modified. Execute again, and then follow up again until it is all working to some level of agreed satisfaction.

The goals are usually fixed. Yes, they too can be modified, but typically only in extreme circumstances. This is a major reason for making sure that the goals are doable, before agreeing to them.

Keep in mind the SMART guidelines on goal making. All goals need to be SMART!

S:	Specific
M:	Measurable
A:	Attainable
R:	Relevant
T:	Trackable

The key word in this example is *attainable*, making the point that you need to make sure that the goal is attainable before agreeing to it. The author observes a lot of unsuccessful sales initiatives strictly due to poor goal setting.

Goals

Goals are deliverables, expectations, and the desired results.

■ Increase sales activity.
■ Close more accounts.
■ Offer better proposals.
■ See more prospects.

These goals are mere rhetoric until they are better defined, as follows:

- Increase sales activity by 9% in 2009.
- Close more accounts, more being defined as an 11% increase by midyear.
- Offer better proposals that result in closed deals increasing by 22% in the 1st Quarter.
- See more prospects. Increase visits each week by a count of two.

Now you have

Goals that are specific, not rhetoric
Goals that are measurable
Goals that are attainable, hopefully, if they are well thought out
Goals that are relevant, because they were successfully "benchmarked"

The goals are trackable because we also developed a software solution to track calls, sales, activity, and successes. This falls directly in line with the SMART theory and practice.

Strategies

Strategies are the mindset agreements on how best to achieve the goals that are agreed to. They are not "executionary concepts," as will be defined by tactics. But they set the stage for the development of the necessary actions that will have to be taken to make it all come together.

A strategy is like creating a road map. It tells us where the places are. It shows our options on how to go from A to B, but it does not tell us how to make the move. Tactics tell us how to make the move.

Strategies need to:
- Make sense
- Fall in line with sales capabilities to make them happen
- Be flexible and easy to modify
- Be encompassing

Strategies can also be compared to a blueprint of a house. It sets the plan on what the contractor needs to do to build the house, but it does not execute the foundation, the framing, the construction, etc.

Tactics

Tactics are the "meat and potatoes." They make it all come together. They are the specific actions that need to be taken that give life to the strategies, that make the goals happen.

Compare it to a war initiative. The president and Congress declare war on a particular country. The goal is to win. The Department of Defense and the commanding generals must come up with a plan, a strategy that will accomplish the goal of winning the war. That strategy is handed off to field officers who execute specific actions and makes things happen. Those things that happen, if all is going right, then makes the strategies work. If the strategies work, then the goals of winning the war should take place. The deliverable is accomplished.

Goals

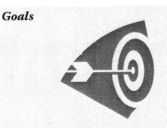

Strategies

Tactics

Goals drive the strategy that drives the tactics ... that
makes the initiatives sought ... happen!

Tactics need to be:

- Coherent
- Flexible
- Simple
- Doable
- Fixable
- Comprehensible at many levels

Sales managers have to wear many hats in this equation. Many times they work to set goals and strategies. That is an excellent position to be in. Having said that, most sales managers are also heavily engaged in managing, supervising, and coaching tactical initiatives. Therefore, having to participate in the goal and strategy setting will give a huge advantage to the sales manager who also now has to execute specific tactics.

Sales managers will typically earn the right to participate in goal and strategy setting when they:

- Become successful sales managers in the eyes of senior management
- Can add value to that process
- Learn the markets, products, and customer base—"ice cold"
- Gain the respect from those setting goals and strategies
- Show the "persistence" to do this
- Manage-up and convince senior management of the value in having them participate in these endeavors

Sales managers who develop a comprehensive understanding of goals, strategies, and tactics and learn to navigate these areas with great delicacy and diligence will create the best opportunity for sales management success.

Managing the Four Corners of the Sales Matrix
Manage-Up, Manage-Down, Manage-In, Manage-Out

These are four sales management concepts that are required of all sales managers to "master" in the quest to be successful:

Managing-Down
Managing-Up
Managing-In
Managing-Out

There is a "matrix" established by the structural nature of most companies. This means that the sales manager will have a boss (managing-up); a salesperson (managing-down); a customer (managing-out); and internal managers, staff, and associates (managing-in) that the sales manager will need to deal with. This typically is accomplished on a day-to-day basis.

A necessary part of the sales management profile is working the four corners of the matrix to assure that the goals, strategies, and tactics set forth can be accomplished.

Manage-Up: This is typically the most difficult aspect of the matrix to manage.

Manage-Down: This is covered throughout this book, and all the areas of concern are discussed and outlined in great detail.

Manage-In: Most companies have other profit and cost centers that operate alongside sales.

Marketing, Finance, Operations

Manufacturing, Legal

Human Resources, R&D, Warehousing

Supply Chain/Logistics, Corporate

> These fiefdoms exist, and as a sales manager you and your sales team will have to interact with all or any one of these departments every given day. The nature of that interaction will go a long way in determining your success as a sales manager.
>
> And we know from experience that people can be easy or very difficult to deal with. People can be beautiful or ugly, easy or stubborn, pig-headed or rational, old-fashioned or contemporary, or just plain assholes.
>
> Your job as sales manager is to make the relationships work, irrespective of personalities, positions, or attitudes. Yours is to lower walls, eliminate barriers, and close gaps. You become a bridge between sales and all the other concerns that make a company work.
>
> Yours is not to judge ... but to make happen.

The hat you wear may one day be as a referee and another day as a negotiator and another day as a diplomat.

We outline several steps to be successful in managing-up:

1. Make sure the goals, strategies, and tactics you are working with have senior management's blessing. This will go a long way in hammering out what might appear to be irresolvable issues with colleagues to your favor. Having senior management support, when they have to make a decision between opposing views—when established early—can mean favorable resolve for you and your team.

2. Work with great visibility and transparency. If everyone in the other departments sees what you are trying to accomplish, they are more likely to be on board when issues arise.

3. Engage your peers and associates from the other departments. Get them involved in what you are doing. They are more likely to support your initiatives when they are engaged in them. Bring them on client, prospect, and business-development calls. Have them participate in trade shows and other sales-oriented activities. It will pay off in spades when you engage their participation.

4. Have your colleagues attend sales management meetings and ask them to prepare presentations and participate in the process.

Their participation and activity will make them feel part of the team.

Keep in mind that, in many organizations, non-sales personnel are jealous and suspicious of sales personnel, who they typically feel are slackers, prima donnas, and make too much money. Your job is to change those feelings and create bridges.

Manage-Out: Making money and managing issues with money are key components of sales management.

Clients and prospects are at the forefront of your responsibilities as a sales manager. Managing-out is the relationships you form with these prospects and clients. In many organizations sales managers manage sales personnel who manage the clients and prospect activities. This places the sales manager in the background. But he or she should not be in the "shadows."

Key prospects and clients should be aware of your existence and, more importantly, the role you might play in assisting them and your salesperson in managing the overall relationship between your two companies.

In attempting to qualify the word "key," one might consider the following issue: The sales manager cannot see all the clients and all the prospects. He or she needs to be selective. The guideline might be to look at the 20/80 rule. This dictates that 80% of the revenue will come from 20% of the accounts. This would be a good starting point in identifying the word "key." For prospects, those that will represent 80% of the new business goals is where you may want to spend your time.

Managing-out must be a combined initiative with your sales personnel. You want to allow them independence, but at the same time be involved. It is a "grey" area that must be treaded lightly. Obviously, more experienced sales personnel will require more delicate involvement. Junior and less experienced sales personnel will allow you to be more aggressive and forthright.

THOUGHTS TO SELL BY...

Obviously I faced the possibility of not returning when I first considered going. Once faced and settled, there really wasn't any good reason to refer to it.

Amelia Earhart

Chapter 3

Globalization and Sales Management

The sales manager of the new millennium must develop additional and more specialized capabilities, talents, and skill sets in an array of areas to meet the issues associated with companies growing their purchasing and business development into foreign markets.

Globalization

Almost every company in one way or another is affected to some extent by globalization, defined as a company's growth into overseas purchasing, manufacturing, foreign supply chains, and export sales to foreign markets. These opportunities present challenges. The challenges or opportunities present a new set of qualifications, as seen in Figure 3.1.

Global issues to be mastered include, but are not limited to, the following:

- Foreign languages
- Diverse cultures
- Currency exchange
- Management of foreign distributors and agents
- Local marketing, promotion and sales differences
- Political risks
- Economic differentiations
- Complicated laws and regulations

- Global risk management
- Vast geographic differences
- Major supply chain and logistics issues
- Packing, marking, and labeling variables
- Dealing with U.S. and foreign customs authorities
- Compliance and security concerns
- Overseas travel
- Time differences
- Major differences in overall sales management and personnel matters
- FCPA: Foreign Corrupt Practices Act

These are but a few of the generic issues that face new sales management initiatives in the New Millennium.

The rest of this chapter presents some thoughts in each one of these areas for the sales manager to bring into his or her business resume to become a more effective leader and to better develop the skill sets and the "art" of sales management.

Foreign Languages

While English may be the chosen language of the world, local language plays a very important part in building close personal relationships with overseas clients. If you want to "raise the bar" with your foreign client, then learn some of the basic verbiage to manage a casual conversation. Obviously, the more you can speak in that language, the better off you will be. But if your company is selling to numerous countries, learning all the languages could prove arduous. Better then to at least learn the rudimentary words and phrases to say:

- Hello and Goodbye
- My name is
- Thank you
- You are welcome
- How, Why, When, Where, How Much
- Days, Dates, Numbers
- Names
- Places
- Typical business phrases that may be unique to your business interests

Keep in mind that, while your customers and trading partners may speak English very well, they will enormously appreciate your having some local language skill sets. And this will go a long way in improving and growing sales and building long-term relationships.

Diverse Cultures

Recognize that many places around the world operate in cultures that are different and pose varied and complex challenges. Recognize that even a country like Great Britain, with whom we have countless similarities, has a "laundry list" of differences. Recognize that a "faux pas" in a cultural issue can cause a "train wreck" to a deal and irreparable harm to a relationship. Take the time to know most of the important and relevant cultural facts about the people and country you are or will be doing business in.

In the Appendix to this book, there is a listing of publications and Web sites this author recommends for readers who wish to research and read further to learn all the key and necessary cultural issues around the world.

Example 3.1

In the United States, purchasing executives have a high degree of brand loyalty that sits above the personal relationship with the salesperson. Meaning in America we buy Coca-Cola. In China, they want Coca-Cola, but they will buy it from Bob the salesman, who represents Coca-Cola. This means that the buying agent in China must feel absolutely comfortable with Bob before he will make the purchase. It may mean a longer time in the decision-making process to allow for relationship building and comfort levels to set in. Showing impatience with a "buyer" in China could be construed as rude and become certain interference in closing the deal.

Example 3.2

In certain Middle Eastern cultures the bonding that takes place over meals, particularly where you are a guest, ranks high in their evaluation of our character. This means you may need to be prepared to eat certain foods that you would normally not eat, so as not to seem rude to your host and show a sign of accepting their full and complete hospitality. Turning down the meal, because it doesn't look right or that it is still moving, could be construed as a sign of rudeness and your unwillingness to participate in their customs and practices.

Example 3.3

In certain Latin American cultures, the "sense of time" is not as critical as it is in certain Western cultures and as it is in America. It is not a case of right and wrong—just different. So if, when setting appointments, meeting deadlines, arranging scheduling, etc., you are not prepared to show a high degree of flexibility, you will soon be disappointed and make for bad feelings. The rule of thumb in most Latin American dealings is to be patient with "time" and exercise abnormal flexibility in deadlines and scheduling. This will work to everyone's benefit and assist in the overall sales process.

Currency Exchange

Currencies fluctuate around the world hourly, daily, and over time. An international salesperson or the salesperson's operational support team must take into consideration this factor when

- Prospecting
- Quoting out proposals
- Determining price points
- Collecting funds
- Carrying out ongoing maintenance and warranty programs

What could happen in an international sale without currency factors being considered is unprofitable transactions and strained relationships with foreign customers. Senior management will also not be happy, and it will jeopardize future international sales initiatives. Maintaining relationships with key international banks can be a useful tool in managing foreign-currency exposures.

In the Appendix there is a list of banks and foreign currency companies that the author recommends as viable options.

Management of Foreign Distributors and Agents

Many corporations manage their foreign sales through agents and distributors located in the countries they have sales in. The success of the sales initiatives in this method of selling will be in direct proportion to how well the agent and distributor is managed. Managing these agents is as much an art as it is a science. The author puts forth six steps to take in managing this area:

1. Learn all you need to know about that market, so that you can be better prepared to evaluate what your agent is advising you and so that you are best prepared to provide the necessary sales support.
2. Meet with the actual customers and create your own relationships with them.
3. Establish comprehensive and contemporary sales/distributor/agency agreements that protect everyone's interests including proprietary rights. Make sure these agreements address when it is time to end the agreement and how the parties move forward in the dissolution.
4. Travel to that country often. Build it into the sales budget. At least twice a year and, if the activity is significant, then at least quarterly.
5. Be careful of local, political, and economic issues that might affect sales into that country or directly affect your sales agent.
6. Control or influence pricing parameters offered to the local customer base. And make sure these fall into the larger strategy of your global business plan.

Local Marketing, Promotion, and Sales Differences

Markets overseas are as diverse as the people and the cultures. In order to be successful in foreign sales management, one must learn the differences in promotion and marketing.

Many of the largest corporations have "macho" war stories on their failed efforts to increase their sales over the course of their global histories. Companies like Parker Pen, Nike, Ford, and Coca-Cola are but a few of many that can offer lots of advice on how to avoid marketing pitfalls in their foreign sales.

Example 3.4

A U.S. company marketed a food product in Mexico. It utilized a translation for describing its taste.

It became embarrassed to find out that the word had different meanings in the various dialects of local regions. In one region what was "hot" connotated a sexual reference.

This was not the intention of the advertisement and proved to be an expensive error.

The lesson here is that mistakes can be costly, and identifying the local nuances is a key ingredient to foreign sales management.

Political Risks

Political risks are those emanating from government or political sources. Confiscation, nationalization, expropriation, deprivation, currency inconvertibility, devaluation, war, strikes, riots, terrorism, and civil commotions are a list of but some of the exposures faced in a global sales initiative. Companies such as General Telephone and Electronics, Occidental Petroleum, Citibank, and Harris Corporation are but a few of thousands of corporations that have had political risks directly affect their overseas sales or operations in an adverse way.

The Appendix provides a detailed overview of political risk exposures.

It is important for sales managers to realize these exposures exist in their overseas sales efforts, and they must be dealt with in a number of ways. One way is through insurance. Another is through risk-management techniques. Most companies have professional risk managers or access to specialized brokerage expertise that can assist them in managing this concern and in maintaining sales development in all countries. Sales managers who work with the risk managers on a consistent and cooperative basis will have better sales results in the long run.

Economic Differentiations

The economy around the world can vary by global region, country, city, or local region and can change quickly or slowly in time. The successful sales manager understands this and creates information flow into any sales effort to make sure the company's interests are protected and that a best-foot-forward approach can be achieved with the sales management team. A sales manager who is a close observer of economic detail in global markets can determine the best time to pull out, the best time to lay low, and when to be aggressive.

The world economy oscillates and runs as a roller coaster does. It changes over time. It has peaks and valleys. There are experts in some companies who watch these changes, and some companies align themselves with consultants, accounting firms, and banks who lend their expertise to this evaluation and decision-making process for the benefit of the sales manager.

The sales manager of the New Millennium has to have a significant inflow of information and expertise—world and local economic conditions being one of them.

Complicated Laws and Regulations

Most sales executives have access to internal legal, regulatory, and compliance personnel whose efforts supplement their responsibilities as sales managers. While many sales managers will leave regulatory and compliance to the experts, all sales managers and their teams have to pay attention to a certain amount of detail, awareness, and facts about compliance that will directly affect their sales and customer service relationships. More times than not, compliance and regulatory positions by management will greatly affect sales opportunities and client relationships.

Compliance can often make or break a deal. Having acknowledged that, it is then an important fact that the more the sales managers engage themselves in the basic compliance and regulatory issues, the better they will serve their prospects and clients and meet corporate goals.

Global Risk Management

Sales managers create opportunities in foreign markets. With these opportunities comes a certain magnitude of risk. The sales managers who proactively identify the risks and work with management to mitigate these risks will place themselves and the company in a most favored position in their global outreach.

The Appendix provides more detail on global risk management.

The basic responsibilities of the sales manager in this area are:

- Assist management in identifying business risks and exposures
- Work with management in mitigating these exposures
- Work with the sales team in awareness training and execution
- Work with prospects and customers (where applicable) in obtaining their cooperation and support, when necessary

Vast Geographic Differences

Selling domestically even across all 50 states has nowhere the vastness and scope of size that the world can bring when we sell internationally. New York to Los Angeles is 3,000 miles. New York to Beijing is over 10,000 miles. And when you are there, it is 13 hours later and already the next day.

Creating sales and managing a sales force on a global basis dramatically increases the size and scope of the supply chain that will be needed to support those sales. You can get on a plane and be in most places in the United States within 5–6 hours. Some international destinations can take two days of travel to visit.

We can do same-day shipping in most places in the United States. Next-day international is a slight potential but not likely.

Major Supply Chain and Logistics Issues

In global logistics, once a sale is made, someone typically will have to move a product from point A to B. International salespeople need to understand the dynamics of global logistics, as very clear and serious roadblocks, hazards, and difficulties await all shipment activity and transactions. Exposures emanating from carriers, weather, and customs authorities—all can play havoc on the simplest of supply chains. The international salespeople that are proactive in the logistics elements of the transaction will place themselves and their foreign customers in a much better place to deal with all the risks.

Packing, Marking, and Labeling Variables

As goods move across borders, every country in the world makes sure that the packing, marking, and labeling on the inbound packages meet local rules and regulations. Some commodities, such as, but not limited to, food products, chemicals, pharmaceuticals, hazardous materials, electronics, etc., may have some very complicated packing and marking requirements. The international salesperson must be aware of these issues and factor any decisions in the sales process with these factors in mind. As much as these rules may present an obstacle, they also can be an opportunity for those companies that are both diligent and prudent and get this logistics responsibility right.

Dealing with U.S. and Foreign Customs Authorities

A sale is not complete until the goods pass through the border, scrutinized and cleared by local customs authorities and moved to their final destination.

Irrespective of the INCO Terms (International Commercial Terms) utilized in the transaction, the seller will have some degree of responsibility to assure that the goods and the accompanying documentation can pass customs muster. Sales personnel who proactively think through these issues will be far better off with a proactive management style than with a reactive style, when issues raise their ugly little heads.

Compliance and Security Concerns

Moving freight internationally has always had compliance and security concerns as part of the whole equation of logistics. The events of 9/11 changed all of that to make security and compliance an integral part of all global transactions and now, even more than ever, there is a whole cadre of regulatory and procedural activities that must take place to engage in global sales (Figure 3.1).

The author wrote a book called *Mastering Import and Export Management*, *AMACOM June 2008*, which covers this subject in greater detail and is a must-read for all international sales executives.

Overseas Travel

Relationship building is a very critical factor in successful international sales. Many senior international sales professionals advocate that foreign buyers typically buy much more on the "relationship" than the specific product or company. This, then, requires travel. You must break bread with your prospects and clients on a regular

Figure 3.1   U.S. Customs and Border Protection (CBP) in action.

basis to develop and foster quality secure relationships. It is much more important typically than in domestic sales.

When creating budgets, the company must anticipate travel costs, which could be significant over the course of several visits to numerous countries. International travel is by no means cheap. Time must also be responsibly allocated, as foreign travel is very time consuming and demanding.

Time Differences

One must recognize that the time differences and days of operation in other parts of the world can be very much different from here in the United States. In Japan, we are 13 hours ahead in time, and it is the next day. At 9 p.m. in New York, it is 10 a.m. in Tokyo. In Frankfurt it is 3 a.m. In Chicago it is 8 p.m. In Rio it is 10 p.m. In Los Angeles it is 6 p.m. So there will be many times you will be up at night or very early in the morning conversing with your trading partners to create sales and handle customer service issues. It can be burdensome and certainly difficult on managing sleep and time issues.

There is not much you can do about these issues, but being aware and practicing time management and a high degree of communications will mitigate many of the overbearing problems with sleep and time.

Domestic Sales vs. International Sales: Major Differences in Overall Sales Management and Personnel Matters

FCPA: Foreign Corrupt Practices Act

With U.S. global supply chains presently expanding their reach to an unprecedented scope and range, adherence to the growing list of security and compliance initiatives stipulated by an ever-increasing number of government agencies has created the need to invest in self-policing. This often falls into the hands of sales executives who are managing global initiatives.

Two twenty-first century hot-button issues, terrorism and corporate accounting fraud, intersect their way into global supply chain issues. There are many parallels between these issues, the challenges they present, and the means to create a proactive check-and-balance system to protect the supply chain from internal and external forces. With all of these new challenges, however, one cannot forget to incorporate preexisting laws into a preventative twenty-first century supply chain compliance action plan. One law that must make its way into the foreground of such a plan is the Foreign Corrupt Practice Act of 1977 (FCPA).

The original purpose of the FCPA was to assign monetary penalties to U.S. companies and individuals found guilty of bribery. This act specifically targets unlawful payments to foreign government officials, politicians, or political parties for the sole purpose of obtaining or maintaining business. The Department of Justice has been the agency responsible for the enforcement of the FCPA and, along with the Securities and Exchange Commission, has levied substantial monetary penalties on many corporations and individuals for their infractions. With Sarbanes-Oxley regulations fully imbedded into the fabric of the corporate American consciousness and Homeland Security mandates to safeguard U.S. interests against terrorism just on the horizon, FCPA regulations may be taking a backseat on a list of priorities for exporters. However, not taking the proper precautions to mitigate the potential risk of exposure to FCPA violations may cause considerable problems for U.S. companies as their growth in the overseas market continues. Violating these laws often results in stiff fines along with possible prison time. Some corporations have found this out the hard way.

Example 3.5

In January 2005, as a result of violating FCPA laws, biotechnology giant Monsanto, headquartered in St. Louis, paid a $1-million fine to the DOJ and a $500,000 fine to the SEC. These penalties represent mitigated amounts due to Monsanto's prompt reporting of the discovery of misconduct and their subsequent cooperation with the investigation pertaining to the actions of their affiliate in Indonesia. Equally important was their willingness to establish internal standard operating procedures (SOPs) and controls, which have become examples for all companies to follow. In December 2004 and February 2005, GE InVision, a subsidiary of

General Electric, settled its cases with the DOJ and SEC. The FCPA violations cost the company a combined total of just under $2 million. The Titan Corporation and Schering-Plough are two additional companies just recently found guilty and fined after being investigated for violations.

A U.S. company conducting business in a foreign country must ensure that none of its employees, subsidiaries, agents, or hired contractors violates FCPA laws. Investing in setting up a monitoring system that performs thorough screenings of all entities conducting business on behalf of the U.S. company is highly recommended. The internal policing of this issue must begin with identifying problematic persons or entities wanting to represent the company in a foreign market. Refusal to submit written compliance to FCPA guidelines, failing to maintain sufficient books or records, requesting payments for an undisclosed third party, or having any relationship with a member of a political party should serve as red flags to exporters. Maintaining an "out of sight, out of mind" mentality or pleading ignorance to situations occurring beyond a self-perceived arm's length will not navigate one through the stormy seas of an FCPA investigation. The concepts of maintaining self-awareness and establishing internal controls repeat themselves over and over again throughout sections of the Sarbanes-Oxley law.

Sales managers applying these principles to a standard operating procedure in order to prevent FCPA violations is a worthy exercise to undertake.

Establishing criteria for self-policing the foreign sales process and supply chain in order to expose potential FCPA issues can start by requiring that all contracts include concise FCPA compliance language. Companies should insist that all payments be made via check or wire transfer while steering clear of any party insisting on using off-shore accounts. Another safeguard that can be applied is to ensure that all applicants for foreign-office positions undergo thorough background checks confirming they do not hold any public office and do not have close ties to a foreign government.

Awareness of corporate responsibilities has become paramount in today's post-9/11, Sarbanes-Oxley world. The government has stepped up its vigilance in protecting both the homeland as well as public confidence in the American business system. U.S. exporters must take the necessary precautions to guard their supply chains from activities that not only pose risks to the United States, but that also jeopardize the sanctity of their company. By taking a proactive and organized approach, a corporation can build a system of checks and balances to simultaneously mitigate risks in areas of security, compliance, and accounting. Maintaining high compliance and security standards within a global supply chain best prepares an organization to not only deal with new twenty-first century government initiatives, but also to safeguard itself against FCPA infractions and other laws from yesteryear.

Globalization has expanded the number of venues that companies are engaged in and, consequently, the number of sales executives working in those venues. They travel all over the world. They are making deals. They commit on the part of the company. They are involved in millions of dollars in negotiations and contracts. And the "web" they cast is getting larger and more complicated as foreign sales and sourcing continues.

The time is now for sales managers to make sure that their teams are aware of the FCPA and are in strict compliance with the law. We recommend the following:

1. Corporations should initiate FCPA guidelines in their sales, Sarbanes-Oxley, or supply chain compliance guidelines.
2. Executives should receive awareness training and develop SOPs for dealing with potential FCPA scenarios that they may become part of.
3. Very specific SOPs should be developed and incorporated into all operating guidelines that ensure compliance.
4. Corporations should initiate internal communications from senior management with nontolerant and strict penalty guidelines.
5. Corporations should conduct annual audits by outside consultants, law firms, and specialists to analyze potential FCPA violations.
6. Corporations should establish internal resources and call centers in the event an executive needs assistance in how to deal with a potential FCPA violation or potential problem situation, without the threat of backlash.
7. Corporations should identify high-risk situations, countries, customers, etc., that may fall to an FCPA violation and proactively mitigate these "hot spots."
8. Corporations should work with internal risk management to determine insurance options and alternative loss-control procedures.

Those sales executives who are proactive in FCPA management will be the ones that avoid the pitfalls and enjoy more successful international trade, freer of government scrutiny and interference.

THOUGHTS TO SELL BY...

We must dare to think "unthinkable" thoughts. We must learn to explore all the options and possibilities that confront us in a complex and rapidly changing world.

James William Fulbright

Chapter 4

Know When to Be the Mother, the Father, the Brother, the Best Friend, or the Boss—What Personality Hat to Wear?

In this chapter the author introduces the concept that there needs to be a decision regarding what "hat" or personality to wear when dealing with personnel in sales. Determining the right fit will determine successful management and problem resolution.

The personality profile of a good salesperson can contain any of the following: selfish, vain, anal, does not like paperwork or detail, outgoing, persuasive, negotiator (thinks he or she is), persistent high achiever, crybaby, good listener, good talker, vile, fragile ego, great personality (maybe), successful profile, know-it-all, experienced (hopefully), and last, but not least, is a good follower.

Yeah, right! Ask any experienced sales manager, and he or she will tell you that the sales staff has all or some of these traits. Ask again and he or she will tell you that, on any given day, many of these traits are good things and on other days they are hopeless behaviors.

Being selfish is, to an extent, a good thing in motivating salespeople. They want to make lots of money. They want to buy expensive cars, nicer homes, and belong to the country club. When motivating them, selfishness is a potentially good trait—to an extent. But when they deal internally with customer service personnel, management, finance, operations, etc., selfishness will be a rude awakening to disharmony and ineffective relationships.

The role of the sales manager is to "guide" the salespeople to manage their selfishness and show discretion when to have it and when to not. The sales manager must often be the corporation's "hallway monitor" for the sales personnel in this regard.

In "mentoring" for the best results of the sales personnel, the sales manager has to utilize an array of behavior techniques that I have identified as "personality hats." What we mean here is that many times the approach in discussing any topic, such as "selfishness," will work best when you think out what personality hat you are going to wear. Do you approach the salesperson as a mother would? Or as a best friend? Or maybe as the boss? Tied into this is the setting of the discussion. Do you talk to him or her over a cocktail, lunch, dinner, or in your office? Do you approach it in a group discussion at a sales meeting?

The venue tied into the personality hat will be critical to obtaining the desired result. This is a critical decision. With some egos, if you approach the subject formally, you could irritate the individual. If you approach it, say, over lunch in passing, more as a "best friend" providing some advice, it might be better received.

I think all sales managers either know from the get-go, or they quickly learn, that each salesperson is unique and that most have fragile egos. How you approach the salesperson is as important as what words you use or the substance of the issue itself.

There are times when you will need to "mother." There will be times you need to "father" a situation. Then there will be times that a very direct approach as the "boss" must be taken. Let's look at an overview.

Which Personality Hat to Wear?

When to Mother?

What we mean here is a softer, more nurturing approach, sometimes used when you have a salesperson who has taken a tough hit—lost a big sale, lost his or her biggest account, just got delivered some bad news, whatever. This might be the time to put on the "mother hat" and console, nurture, and hold his or her hand.

Personally, I am not a big fan of "mothering." In most instances it can be addicting and offer no real constructive counsel to the salesperson. But having said that, there have been a few times that I have needed to "mother," and it should be in every sales manager's coffer of techniques to deal with staff, when appropriate.

When to Father?

What we mean here is a more logical, straightforward approach. This approach fits certain sales personalities who relate to dominant figures, who are very respectful of authority, and who need a senior figure in their lives. They are often good followers, logical, and pretty reasonable individuals. They typically respond to constructive criticism and accept change more easily. They are fairly organized, so providing an "agenda" of what steps need to be addressed or taken will probably work well.

When to Be the Best Friend?

What we mean here is an approach that won't be offensive. This is an approach best used when you have a person who is more sensitive to criticism or change or when you have someone who likes to socialize and conduct business in an easier, more relaxed environment. It can work well when you have a salesperson whose ego prefers an "equal" providing advice as suggestions. While this approach may have value, one would have to be very careful in dispensing it in this venue, so as to make sure the advice, counsel, or suggestions are taken seriously and will be accomplished.

When to Be the "Boss"?

What we mean here is an approach that applies when the issue must be dealt with now, with less room for change over time. This approach is certainly favored by the author. You are the "boss," so you need to always represent yourself as such. The other approaches are exceptions allowed because of the various personalities and egos associated with sales personnel.

The author prefers the "boss" approach because it keeps you in a senior position when dispensing your points. It provides you with a "hammer" when you might need one to make a point. Within the conversation, you might utilize the other personality hats, when apropos. They can be utilized in and out of the conversation when you need to change your approach, tone, demeanor, or voice inflection.

Some Examples

The different personality hats can assist you in taking variable approaches to making your points throughout the meeting and to give you advantages in the discussion or negotiation. Overall, the critical issue for the sales manager is to learn the personalities of his or her sales staff and identify the circumstances at hand—and then apply whichever personality hat will get the job done.

The importance of managing the "approach" to an issue, motivational matter, or a problem with a salesperson emanates from the following:

- All salespeople are not the same.
- Their personalities and approaches to relationships will vary greatly.
- They typically have fragile egos.
- Being sales oriented, their disposition tells them to be cautious when approached about issues.
- They are continually "negotiating."
- Good salespeople are all from Missouri; they must be "shown" to believe.
- Once "onboard," once they are a "believer," they are usually loyal and committed.
- They hate criticism about themselves or about how they sell.

Hopefully, you agree with those descriptions of most salespeople. If so, then the "approach" you take to effect change, provide criticism, or otherwise is as important as the substance of the point you want to make. While this is true in all areas of management, I find it more relevant with sales personnel because of the need to keep them so continually motivated and upbeat.

Example 4.1

An Example That Does Not Go Well

You have a life insurance and securities saleswoman named Karen, high achiever, seasoned veteran. For the last six months her sales have been slipping. In her 12-year tenure, at no point has she ever dipped like this. She has a huge ego. She won salesperson of the year three times and thinks she is the very best at what she does. She dresses very nicely, is attractive, and is an A+ personality type. She has some unconventional sales approaches that have worked for her in the past, but with some of the new product lines, these approaches are just not working. She has boasted about "writing a book" on her sales style in many evening cocktail conversations with her colleagues and you.

You have an edict from senior management that requires certain sales quotas to be maintained and to show corrective action when sales dip. Karen needs to be approached. And you need to obtain a deliverable, the deliverable being that you need her to consider alternative ways to sell, without getting her so pissed off that she will refuse to consider change or lose motivation.

So which approach do you take? Which "personality hat" do you wear?

You decide, because of timing, to be the "boss." You call her into the office and you outline for her a scenario showing her how the numbers are falling for the last six to seven months. You point out to her that her unconventional methods, which you have always taken exception to, are not working. The results are very evident.

You then proceed to outline a corrective course of action that will absolutely provide a turnaround in her sales results.

During the meeting you notice her turning a little red in the face. Eye contact has been minimized. Her demeanor tells you she is only partially listening, and she allows two disruptions to occur during the meeting from cell phone calls.

You leave the meeting with a commitment from her to make the changes, but you know as a sensibility that it was not heartfelt or too convincing. Three months later the sales are still down as she resigns. She advises that there is another life insurance and financial services company that is more in line with her way of producing.

Not a good scenario. You just lost a quality salesperson and to a competitor—a double whammy.

Another Way of Handling This Situation

You put on your "best friend" hat. You invite her to lunch. During lunch you mention the decline in sales, inadvertently. She nods and says she is trying hard but no one is buying the new product line. You sympathize with her. You tell her that you had a similar problem ten years earlier, when you were selling and not managing. You boost her ego up by saying that even the best sluggers have a slump.

You then put on the "big brother" hat. You ask her why some of the other salespeople have been selling the same product. She says she is not sure why. You start a series of questions to her. You say, "Let me get your expert opinion on this." You say you would appreciate her evaluating the approach that some of the other salespeople have been taking.

This conforms to her ego and her sensibilities. You are appreciative of her input and experience. You desire her thought process. Simultaneously, while working with her ego, she is now observing what the other sales personnel are doing that work for them. She is learning a potentially new sales process while evaluating this for you.

Your deliverable does not have to be achieved in one meeting. You tell her to evaluate the process for a few days and reschedule a meeting with her early next week. At that time, you want her to give you her view of the different sales approach and to advise you on whether other sales personnel should consider it.

Next week comes. She—on her own—has decided to give the new process a try and tells you this. She advises that she has modified it a little and actually feels like it is working after a few conversations with some of her prospects and accounts. At your meeting, she recommends that all sales personnel should consider the new process and she offers to assist in any way she can.

Three months go by and her sales have steadily increased and a win-win scenario has been created.

Evaluation

You evaluate your approach—Monday quarterback your actions. You spoke to her first as a friend, then as a big brother. Neither threatened her ego or sensibilities. You then approached the entire subject by asking her opinion on the new sales process and having her evaluate it and observe it, independent of it, as a demand. You were interested in her expert opinion. She liked that and was open to it.

Clearly the second approach worked with much more favorable results. The deliverables were achieved and even possibly more. Karen appreciated your approach because you wanted her opinion. You satisfied her ego and achieved the desired results and more.

I want you as the reader to understand that the most important point here is that a variable approach, utilizing some very basic instincts, worked well.

You were sensitive to her personality and her individual sensibilities. You put forth a nonthreatening idea and let her work it out over a few days and come to her own conclusions. There was no browbeating or bossy approach.

At the end of the day you were considerate in thinking out not only the substance of what needed to get accomplished, but how best to accomplish that within the realm of the personality you were dealing with.

It sounds complicated, but it was not. It applied an approach that worked for everyone. The deliverable was achieved with the least amount of collateral damage.

Example 4.2

An Example That Does Not Go Well

Bob is a salesman who is also an engineer by background. His largest account has raised some service concerns directly to senior management and not through Bob. There will be financial consequences to the company as a result of the issues.

The customer felt as though Bob was part of the problem, not by being culpable on the issues, but by not addressing the client's concerns when red flags had been raised.

Bob is a long-term employee with 26 years invested with the company. He is organized, diligent, and articulate.

You do a preliminary evaluation of the situation, and while Bob is usually on top of his clients issues, he did miss the ball on this one. Your deliverable is to reprimand Bob and advise him that the loss will come out of his commissions and to get him to take some basic customer service training classes, which he has been reluctant to take, as he feels this is beneath him.

You set an appointment with him. When you meet, he is very upset, as he just found out about his client's call direct to senior management and the potential loss of revenue to the company and his loss of commissions. You decide to take a "motherly" approach. You console him. You reiterate his value to the company and state that this was just an aberration. Your focus is dealing with his emotions of feeling bad and being so upset.

He is still so upset during the 40-minute meeting that you soften the information flow by saying that there will be some financial consequences to him as a result of the problem, but that you would have another conversation with management and see if something could be done to mitigate the commission loss. You decide not to address the training resolve, as you think that will push him over the edge. You hold that off to another meeting in a few weeks.

When a few weeks go by and he is a little more relaxed, you now drop the bad news that his commissions will be lowered and that customer service training starts next week. He is so infuriated that it affects his entire performance and attitude in the office. It takes almost 12 months before the situation becomes settled and the relationship with Bob and the company is back on track.

The deliverable was never really achieved, and lots of pain and anguish was felt along the way.

Another Way of Handling This Situation

You decide the best option is to wear a "hat of the boss and maybe the father" in handling this matter.

You send a memo to Bob outlining the issues in brief and make an appointment with him, within 48 hours. Bad news should be dealt expeditiously. You start out the conversation with the fact that he has a long favorable tenure with the company and overall he has been a great staff member and asset to the organization. You then tell him to what extent you have investigated the chain of events and the issues at hand.

You ask him to offer his thoughts on the matter. He accepts responsibility of not seeing the red flags and offers that he thought he could handle the matter without going elsewhere in the company. He also did not sense just how upset the client was.

You review with him his thought process and offer to him what steps he could have taken to avoid this entire fiasco.

You outline for him what could have been an alternative course of action. You seek his acknowledgment and confirmation of same.

You stress that he is not working in a vacuum and that he has you to depend upon, as well as the support of senior management and other expertise within the organization. You stay with this until you feel for certain that he gets the point.

Now you "father" him. You reiterate firmly how important education and training was for him to get his engineering degree and how that training produced a nice career and livelihood. You then draw a line of similarity between the customer service training he has now to take and the continuation of his career and livelihood. "Hey, Bob, while you may know all this stuff already, a refresher may just lift the spirits." You then outline a strategy to get back the lost business and to eliminate the loss of revenue and commissions. Bob buys into the plan and agrees to do his part.

Two months later, Bob has taken the training and actually admits learning a few things. He has obtained back about 50% of the original loss and should get back the balance by year's end.

Evaluation

You clearly see the benefit that a direct, no-nonsense approach worked with the personality of Bob. Coddling made you feel better. It was less confrontational and less intimidating, but it was a short-term benefit and a long-term loss. It did not achieve the desired results.

The second approach fit more in line with Bob's engineering background and his more-logical mindset. You tailored your approach and put on the right personality hats. The benefits and the deliverables were more easily obtained, and a win-win scenario was achieved for all.

Example 4.3

John is a seasoned salesperson in your software management company. However, he has only been on board for six months. His promise was high. He said he had a following and, given the right technical and customer service support, he could double his sales from his predecessor company.

In his first six-month review, his numbers are only 25% of his semi-annual goals, and the pipeline of short-term opportunities is very limited. You meet with

John and decide to wear the "boss and mentor" hat. You have John control the meeting indirectly by having him explain how he is doing. You ask questions only, with very few comments. You make sure that the fault does not lie internally with technical support and customer service.

John offers no concrete explanation. He seems to be all over the place with excuses and rationale. And John offers no sure resolve. You are confident in John's capability and know he needs some direction and heading. You tell him that you will meet again in three weeks and ask him to prepare an outline of what went wrong and, more importantly, what he needs to do to get it back on track. You are letting him control and manage his own analysis and recovery.

Before he goes, you reinforce his strengths and commit to your confidence and faith in his capabilities. Before he leaves the meeting, you advise him to look at some areas of how he handled the transition communications from his anticipated following, which was not there for him. You have him review the differences and benefits of his new company. You suggest that he sit with a few of the other ten-ured salespeople to see how they manage their sales initiatives. You even offer to make some arrangements for him to go on some joint sales calls. You also accept some of the responsibility for the poor showing here in the beginning. You men-tion that you could have been more attentive, maybe should have made some more joint sales calls and coordinated some better internal support. You part in a friendly, constructive, and upbeat way.

During the three-week period before your meeting with John, you note that he appears busy, is certainly working on his assignment and interacting with the other sales representatives, and more importantly, a new account from his prior company is now on board.

When you meet in that third week, the results are excellent. First of all, John accepts responsibility for the initial slow start and offers some very specific areas that he could have done much better in. More importantly, he outlines ten very specific steps he will be taking to improve his making his goals. You review the ten steps, which you modify a bit, and add two more additional steps that will really make the action plan complete.

You reinforce an enthusiastic departure by emulating confidence and success. You offer your continued support and assistance and suggest another follow-up meeting in 2–3 weeks. As you approach year end, John is ahead of his goal and the situation is under control.

Evaluation

You were successful here because you exercised patience with a seasoned sales executive. You allowed him time to review what he needed to do better and allowed him to construct his resolution. You continued to be upbeat and optimis-tic and kept his sense of confidence in good working order.

Many people do not transition well. Even the very best salesperson could struggle with bringing over accounts and successfully selling from a new platform. Getting involved and aiding in transitional management issues works very well in this case.

THOUGHTS TO SELL BY...

There are many spokes on the wheel of life. First, we're here to explore new possibilities.

Ray Charles

Chapter 5

Mentoring and Developing the Skill Sets of Your Sales Staff

The most critical goal of your sales staff is to maintain existing accounts, grow them when possible, and produce new business. Their best opportunity to achieve these results is when they possess the necessary skill sets.

Sales Skill Sets

Skill sets for sales personnel will vary by company and product/service, but most experts will agree that there are seven necessary skill sets for sales excellence:

- Listening skills
- Emulating a professional persona
- Emulating a caring and friendly persona
- Negotiation skills
- Persistence
- Motivation
- Excellent communication skills

If we agree these are the critical sales skill sets, then we need to develop a strategy to make sure our sales staff has these skills and that they are continually being enhanced.

Sales Skills Development Strategy

1. Assess both team and individual capabilities in all areas.
2. Benchmark the capabilities.
3. Meet with, communicate with, and obtain both team and individual acknowledgment of their strengths and weaknesses, with a focus on the areas requiring improvement.
4. Develop and agree with the team and the individuals just what they will be doing to enhance their shortfalls. Motivation is a key ingredient and moves them into a solid direction.

The need for a sales skill development strategy might become apparent following your assessment that a number of deals that should have closed have not. All the reasons for the company to buy from you are there, but no favorable result. And this is a consistent outcome. The assessment clearly points to a lack of skill sets in closing, which leads to the development of "negotiation skill-set development."

The team and the individuals "buy-in" to the issue and agree to accept some in-house training for three days paid for and delivered by the sales manager and the organization.

In some individual cases, external and more comprehensive negotiation skill-set training could be delivered. The use of external third-party consultants and training companies could pay off in spades here. The American Management Association (www.amanet.org), Dale Carnegie (www.dalecarnegie.com), Karrass (www.bothwin.com), and The World Academy (www.theworldacademy.com) are all excellent options in this regard.

Once the training is accomplished, a follow-up system must be in place to determine if it is working. Sometimes this training is a "first step" and has to be considered a work-in-process.

Obviously, an increase in retention and sales will be a measurable result, but the sales manager needs to be assured that the reason for the results is attributable to the training and not from other reasons. Only then will you truly know that the training has been effective.

The motivation utilized here to get the individual and the team to actively and openly participate in the training is based on the same incentives utilized to motivate their sales—money, security, and job advancement.

Every sales manager reviews his or her sales personnel on a usual and determined basis. What needs to be done is to incorporate this list of skill sets in the review. Next to each skill set is a rating from 1 to 5 on how that salesperson is doing in this area along with the prior rating and where he or she is now. A continual dialogue in each skill-set area will help promote a healthy and beneficial communication on where the salesperson stands individually and set the stage for actions on improvement.

Excelling in Customer Service: Best Practices

In many companies, the sales department is also responsible for customer service or certainly interfaces with it. Irrespective of whether sales directly manages it, it certainly has a direct responsibility to make sure that the customers are served well and all their day-to-day needs are met.

When customer service reports into sales, it is easier to manage. When customer service reports into another operating unit, sales will only be an influence, so certain controls are less likely to happen.

In many companies, sales personnel are first responders to customer needs. In other companies, once the account is on board, the customer will contact customer service directly.

When a problem occurs, many times the customer will call the salesperson requesting his or her involvement to provide a quick resolution. At this time, depending upon how a company is structured, the salesperson may struggle to get customer service to respond in a certain way. This is when the manager of sales and customer service will work closely together to come up with a mutually agreed solution that protects the client's issues and maintain the account satisfactorily.

The ultimate key to the relationship between sales and customer service, irrespective of which way it is structured, is to make sure it is delivering a first-class product and service to the customer—any way possible, anytime.

Here are some suggestions to establish a Best Practices in Customer Service Program in your organization:

1. Make sure you keep your promises. It is perfectly okay to promise the client the Moon. But make sure you deliver the Moon! And nothing less!
2. Maintain responsible and timely communications. Clients know things can go wrong, but at those times it is critical to communicate responsibly and timely. The client needs to know what the status is and how you are taking steps to mitigate the situation. Good communication is a cornerstone of any quality customer service program.
3. Always deliver value added. This means doing more. This means taking steps to differentiate your service and product from your competition in a way noticeable to your customer.
4. Make sure the staff servicing the customer is top shelf. The "A" Team mentality must be in place. That means that they have all the necessary skill sets, experience, and capabilities that are required to deliver first-class service.
5. Make sure the client sees a "team" initiative. When clients understand that a vendor/provider has depth, backup, and layers of qualified staff, they tend to feel more confident in the overall relationship. While only one person may be the key customer service contact, the depth of the team is a very critical

sensibility to the customer that they want to feel good about. So take every opportunity in sales to show the depth of the organization, when possible.

6. When customer service personnel are provided rewards, incentives, and ownership of business, they will tend to work better and more effectively on behalf of your organization in servicing client needs.

7. Engage customer service personnel in all aspects of handling and managing the client. Bring them out to visit with clients. Have them involved in client strategies and management meetings that discuss client and customer service issues. Listen to your customer service representatives. They have the day-to-day relationship with the client and can often best offer input into problem solving or those things that will make the overall relationship better. They have opinions and can often provide invaluable insight. They also have feelings, and engaging them in the process will go a long way in gaining their dedication to quality client services.

8. Do not let complacency slip into client relationships. Be very proactive in talking with customers and asking, "How are we doing?" Perform customer surveys on the relationship. Never take the client for granted. Do not be arrogant or condescending, and show your gratefulness and respect every opportunity you can.

9. Engage the customer in your business. Many times, informed customers are appreciative of what your business is about, the things you have to deal with in delivering products or services, and the challenges you face. The customers will value two-way communications and the development of a "partnership" mentality. They often can provide assistance and support in difficult times. And many times they can even bring solutions to the table.

10. Collaboration between customers and providers/vendors make the very best of relationship cornerstones.

THOUGHTS TO SELL BY...

A powerful idea communicates some of its strength to him who challenges it.

Marcel Proust

Chapter 6

Motivational Techniques and Enhancing Bottom-Line Results

Some sales managers believe that motivation is one of the more difficult areas of sales management. The following guidelines will help dispel that notion. One can learn that motivation is easier than one believes and also can be a lot of fun.

Why We Need to Motivate

As sales managers, we are responsible to a bottom line. Assisting us in this goal is our sales team. Obtaining their performance is best achieved with strategic motivation programs and initiatives. When motivation is part of the sales regimen, then the best opportunity to meet goals is reached.

Two Types of Motivation

The two types of motivation can be characterized by individual and team. It is very important to take notice that the difference in approach to the two motivational sides will be key to a successful sales program. Techniques in both will be reviewed later in this chapter.

A successful sales program will require the sales team pulling together and pulling individually. If you have ten salespeople and only two reach their goals, which might not be enough to meet the overall team sales goals, then failure has occurred.

There is a "balance" that must be reached for both the team and the individuals making up the team. Goals are first set for the team, then for the individuals. This order rolls over to motivation as well. A sales manager designs sales incentives and first motivates the team. Then he or she designs incentives and strategies for the individual.

It is like handling a professional baseball team before the game. "Boys, in order to win tonight we have to hold them to only 1 to 2 runs and we have to score at least 4 to 5. We have to have a very strong defense. Then our batting must come out strong in the early innings, as their relief pitchers are top shelf. The infield must be quick and cover the bases well. The outfield must play short and back up the infield, as we know they are short but consistent ground-ball hitters."

All of this speaks to the team. Now the coach personalizes the message. "Bob (the pitcher), we expect you to play for 7 innings. You must play the fastball and move them out swinging. Terry (1st baseman), your defense of first base will determine our success tonight, as we know they will have a lot of infield hits and you will see a lot of activity. José (shortstop), we know the majority of their hits will come at you. You need to be aggressive and throw that ball to 1st, ASAP! Donald (lead-off batter), we expect you to produce for us and get on base right from the start. Eddie (batting clean-up), Don will get on base and we expect you to bring him home. Remember, they leave the pocket open between center and left field. You also have a career RBI goal that could be reached tonight. Boys, remember if we win tonight we will make the playoffs. That was our original goal. Let's not forget what this means to us individually, as a team, to our club, the fans, and the city—and in our pocketbooks. Let's go get 'em!"

That entire story addresses the thought process of team vs. individual goals that most of us can relate to.

Team Motivation

We need to set certain motivation criteria for the entire sales force. These can be in the form of:

- Contests
- Rewards
- Recognition

Recognize that these will not work for everyone, and should they fail, they can cause some resentment and do some harm.

Team motivation activities must be well thought out and apply to everyone, as much as possible. The underlying purpose of team motivation techniques is to build camaraderie and team spirit—for everyone to pull together and ultimately to assist in achieving sales goals.

Example 6.1

A car dealership needs to have a strong 4th Quarter and increase sales by 30%. Typically, year-end sales drop below other quarter sales. The buying public seems to lose interest in buying during the Christmas and Hanukkah holidays, and most buyers wait for the New Year to make that purchase.

Dan, the sales manager, has been directed to increase sales for the 4th Quarter by 30%, a goal he has accepted with trepidation, but he has been promised a $100,000 sales override if the initiative was successful. He has also felt the pressure of having the General Management Position available to him, if he can succeed here.

He has six seasoned sales representatives on his team and one rookie with about a year's experience.

The seasoned staff is focused on its sales and not the rookies which is a key reason as a group it is off its mark.

The sales manager provides goals for each seasoned salesperson and rookie. The goals include the caveat … that they all must be at 80% of their goals for incentives to be paid, including the rookies. If all members of the team do not meet their goals, their incentives are dramatically reduced.

This gives a more meaningful carrot to the seasoned sales personnel to bring the rookies along, and make sure they succeed as well.

THOUGHTS TO SELL BY...

It is not once or twice but times without number that the same ideas make their appearance in the world.

Aristotle

Chapter 7

Case Studies in Sales Management Problem Solving

Case 1

You are a new sales manager of 2 months, with seven sales associates. Some of them were your peers before your promotion, and you are now struggling with discerning your new management role and being their friend. How do you handle this?

This situation can be addressed as outlined in steps 1–6:

Resolution Step 1

Develop a mindset that you earned the position by performance and that senior management saw something in you and not in them. So do not be apologetic or sheepish about the promotion.

Additionally, recognize that the promotion may potentially change your relationship with them, forever. You are now a senior colleague, their boss—the person who influences and helps determine their futures, their livelihoods, and their careers.

When you accept the new management position, you recognize that these relationships may change and that they may never come back to where they were before, usually no matter what.

Resolution Step 2

Make sure that your former peers become allies in your promotion. Explain to them that you are now in a position of influence and some power and have a good chance to make some of the changes that you all bitched about two months earlier, when you were all on the same side of responsibility.

Resolution Step 3

Engage your former peers in your initiatives to make the whole sales experience better for all. The more they "participate" in the sales process and share in your responsibilities, your thought process, and eventually the changes that come about, the easier it will be to "manage" them.

Resolution Step 4

As quickly as possible, be of value to them. The sooner they "feel" your presence in a positive way and realize that you can make a positive impact on their sales, their lives, etc., the sooner they will accept your management role. You will gain their trust and confidence. A good manager always has the trust and confidence of the staff.

Resolution Step 5

Be straightforward, direct, and honest. Explain your apprehensions. Explain your goals. Tell them how they are still part of a bigger agenda and that although this change may be uncomfortable for both parties at first, over time they will see why you were chosen and turn their mind-set to approval and eventual support.

Misrepresentations at this point are deadly in relationship building.

Resolution Step 6

Be quick to praise, but not with so much vigor that it shows pretensions. Be substantive and communicate clearly and positively when things go right. When things go wrong, you need not be sheepish or too delicate. Think out beforehand the best way to say what you need to say, without being too aggressive or offensive.

Clearly state the facts, the issues, and the chain of events. Present a scenario that leaves little room for banter or debate. Establish "a same page" approach. You may want to send some "shots across the bow" first, before coming too hard—more diplomacy, less military posture.

Case 2

You are a new sales manager of 6 months, with 10 sales associates. Two of them are more senior than you by over 10 years, and you are now struggling with their intimidation and lack of a cooperative attitude. You need to produce results, and this is a major obstacle to success. What can you do?

Take this in steps:

Resolution Step 1

Develop the mindset that you are the manager and eventually they must follow your lead and direction. Gain confidence that senior management saw something in your performance to make you the boss. You earned what you got.

Resolution Step 2

Older, more seasoned personnel greatly appreciate:

- Praise
- Involvement
- Stroking
- Recognition of their experience

So do it! Do all four. It will be amazing how quickly you will gain their favor.

Resolution Step 3

Use their experience to a mutual advantage. If they have something to offer, such as helping out some new sales personnel, or lecturing/teaching some newbies, etc., then engage them. You will be very surprised how their attitude will quickly turn around when they feel appreciated and of value.

Keep in mind that your promotion passed them by. They might not be mad at you. You are only the brunt of their frustration at senior management that you are now representing.

They really do have something to offer—experience. Take advantage of it, and it will demonstrate your leadership in getting them on board to your management.

Resolution Step 4

As quickly as possible, be of value to them. The sooner they "feel" your presence in a positive way and realize that you can make a positive impact on their sales, their lives, etc., the sooner they will accept your management role.

You will gain their trust and confidence. A good manager always has the trust and confidence of the staff, no matter how old or experienced they are.

Case 3

Your company sells software to the pharmaceutical industry. Sales have witnessed a yearly 15% growth under your watch for the prior 5 years. In the last 10 months, sales have been flat, and senior management is openly unhappy, and you are feeling pressure. You need to turn things around pretty quickly. You have 12 seasoned sales reps, who are scratching their heads.

What can you do?

The steps we take are:

1. Assess the market and the industry, and draw quick conclusions as to what is going wrong. Some might consider a SWOT analysis—Strengths, Weaknesses, Opportunities, and Threats. This can involve senior management, your 12-person sales team, colleagues from other areas in the company, and the possible use of outside consultants.
2. From the analysis, develop an action plan outlining steps, time frames, and expected results.
3. Present this plan to management to help settle their immediate concerns and to get them to "buy-in." Their "buy-in" is critical on a number of fronts:
    - You may need their support on internal changes or infrastructure needs.
    - Monies may be required to effect certain changes.
    - Their support may be a catalyst for change to make the action plan successful.
4. Delegate the actions necessary to the entire sales staff to help execute the plan. Make sure each sales associate knows what he or she has to do and what the goals are.
5. Meet often to review the plan and tweak as required or as may be necessary.
6. Run sales initiatives to promote higher levels of activity, persistence, and closing of deals.
7. Reach out to existing clients and prospects. Run promotions and meet customer needs to a higher level.
8. Find ways of adding value to your products and services.
9. Develop more cost-effective solutions in your sales and supply chain relationships between vendors, suppliers, and clients.
10. Set short-term goals that can immediately boost sales, but plan a longer-term strategy for future initiatives.

Case 4

The sales staff is struggling with an increasing number of complaints coming from existing clients on customer service issues. Customer service reports to operations, which is not under your control. Clients are being lost. Sales staff is very upset. And the word is leaking out into the market that your company can't deliver on its promises.

You need to bring resolve these problems quickly. How?

Resolution Step 1

The clients need to be met with and surveyed, and the situation must be analyzed to identify specific service failures that can be utilized to effect internal change. Assure the clients that change will happen immediately.

Resolution Step 2

Come up with an agenda/action plan that will provide immediate relief and a longer-term plan for longer-term results. The last thing you want is a continuation of the problem.

In short, the leak needs to be repaired, and then the foundation needs to be reconstructed to ensure no more leaks.

Resolution Step 3

Senior management needs to be involved, as effecting change into other corporate fiefdoms will take their leadership and authority. Senior management must work with you in reviewing your plan of action and agreeing to put it into place.

Resolution Step 4

Engage the managers of customer service, operations, warehousing, manufacturing, etc., where the problem may be originating. Make sure they accept responsibility to some extent. Tell them what you plan on doing differently to work with them. Solicit their comments and suggestions. Work "with them" to come up with a mutual solution. Their "buy in" is also critical for success. Keep saying, "This works for our mutual interest." Any resistance should be overcome by the senior management involvement and authority.

Resolution Step 5

Keep in close contact with your customers. Make sure they know you are concerned, and make sure they see the changes and know the changes are working. Tweak where necessary.

In a positive way, keep in their face as the problem works its way through. Mitigation and recovery will go a long way in regaining the confidence of the client. Also provide feedback internally to make sure that those involved are aware of the success. Be generous with praise.

Case 5

A female salesperson—a single parent of two young kids who has been a good performer over the last three years—has sales that are beginning to slide. For the last six months the new business and some of the renewal is not happening, as planned out earlier in the year. Everyone is becoming frustrated. She also seems a little stressed and off center.

What do you need to do?

Some thoughts:

- Meet with her privately. Stress how valuable she is to the organization. Emphasize your concern for the numbers and, more importantly, your commitment to her and a mutual resolution. This should be a "feel good" session. Have her walk away feeling good. There is no need to bring closure or to resolve the problem at this point. All you are trying to do is to frame the concern, the commitment to resolve, and set up another meeting for a day or two later. Ask her to think of what she and you can do to bring the problem to a favorable resolution.
- At the next meeting, frame the problem again. Obtain a clear consensus as to what the issues are. In this case, the issue seems to be her problems with child care and her "single parent" concerns. Her time as a parent conflicts with her time in sales, and she is stressed because most of the burden is on her. She has little support from hubby or family/friends and is beginning to feel a lot of pressure.
- A potential solution might be to temporarily change her hours to be more accommodating to her parental responsibilities as a single parent. You might also consider a possible realignment of some of her responsibilities, allowing her more time to fulfill her parental obligations. Obviously, there will be compromises made for the short term with hope and trust that it will pay off in the long run.
- Attempt to see if some of her work could be done at home. Assist in setting up a home office, allowing her to complete her tasks in an environment that presents fewer parental conflict issues.
- A possible realignment of clients may present a different scheduling opportunity for her that might work best for her and the accounts.

The key is to be patient, flexible, and accommodating when it will work out for mutual benefit. Actions may need to be tweaked as the situation moves ahead.

Having regular meetings with her to evaluate the success of the actions is very important to a successful resolution of this problem.

Case 6

Your company sells freight services to Fortune 1000 companies. You have three regional sales directors, and each of them has from six to eight individual sales executives. The company has a stable sales force with many tenured staff. All seemed to be well situated. However, in the last 9 months you have lost one sales director and three sales executives to numerous and various competitors. Now, accounts are being lost and you are faced with two serious issues: loss of revenue and low sales morale. The threat of losing more sales staff and accounts is looming. Senior management has expressed concern over your management style and leadership skills for what is happening now. This problem needs to be resolved—directly, quickly, and without fail.

Some thoughts:

1. Sometimes success breeds complacency, particularly over periods of time. Perhaps the compensation program is not contemporary or the services are not competitive, making new sales more difficult.
2. Whatever the issues are, they need to be investigated quickly and identified so that resolutions can be implemented.
3. You may want to interview the staff that has left, if that is possible. Certainly interview the existing staff to see how they feel.
4. Interview all clients, vendors, and staff from other departments, such as customer service and operations. You are on a mission to take in as much information as possible in a very short time.
5. Talk with senior management and mentors. Get some good old "sage" advice and counsel. Perhaps even bring in an outside sales consultant to do some benchmarking and comparison reviews.
6. Make sure that all of the existing directors and sales staff know that you are doing this review and that changes (for the better) will be forthcoming. This will help stem continued loss of personnel.
7. You may want to create an action plan for the short term to stabilize the situation, followed by a longer-term plan to provide a more solid platform for extended resolution.
8. Make a serious attempt to get back one of the sales staff who left. This would go a long way in mitigating the flight of sales personnel, presently and into the future.
9. Engage the existing sales directors and staff to provide recommendations and input into all of the resolutions. When they are "participating," they are more likely to feel part of the team and respond more favorably. In my experience,

many times large flights of personnel are caused by a disconnect between management and staff. So reconnect by having them participate. It will be appreciated and make the resolve go more easily.

10. Don't buy loyalty back, but it is okay to offer new and varied incentives as a motivational technique in stabilizing the loss of sales personnel. Salespeople are typically motivated by incentives, but they could be very focused on new resolutions if the outcomes work more favorably in their way.

The resolution strategy must be managed daily to ensure that the actions are working or determine whether they need to be modified, tweaked, or changed. The situation obviously is tenuous, so diligence is very important.

Case 7

Your sales staff is having difficulty in closing deals. There seems to be a lot of activity and proposals, quotes, etc., but not too many new accounts. You are only 20% toward your goal with 3 months left until year end. No one is happy.

What can you do?

Resolution Step 1

You need to revise the goal. If you are only 20% toward a year-end goal with 3 months left, it is unlikely to happen. Create a new 3-month goal with significant results projected. Then promise to make up the overall annual deficit within the next 6 months of the following year. Senior management should buy into that proposal.

Resolution Step 2

You will need to assess why deals are not closing. Potential culprits include the following:

- Pricing
- Competitive service and value-added deficits
- Lack of qualified closing skills
- Poor proposals from a "quality communicative" benchmark
- Lack of quality relationship with buyers
- Not selling to the decision maker
- Failure to convince prospect to "buy-in"
- Extraneous issues

Pricing

Is it possible that your pricing is not contemporary? When was the last time you "benchmarked" your pricing strategies? Have you spoken with existing clients to see where your pricing agreements stand compared with competitors knocking on their doors? This can be a very critical issue. Pricing generates a lot of "buzz" in the decision-making process of most buyers and purchasing executives.

It also affects your company's profitability. Unless a decision has been made to run a "loss leader" initiative, then pricing will usually be the single most important factor in both the interest of the seller and the buyer. Therefore it is critical to go in the first time with pricing pretty close to what you need to offer to close the deal.

This takes relationship and negotiation prowess. You need to know what your "price points" are. Price points are the two numbers in pricing that are critical to successful negotiation. One price point is the desired price from a supplier perspective. This typically affords the sales company reasonable profit margins. The other price point is the lowest price you will offer to either obtain or maintain the business. This number typically offers unfavorable profit margins. The attitude here is that you do not want to lose the business and, at this number, you will be a little ahead or break even.

In a "loss leader" scenario, the supplier is typically agreeing to a loss, but only to gain market share, with some future date in mind that will allow a price correction to more reasonable profit margins.

It would be typical that senior management would be engaged in price-point setting, particularly in the areas where desired profit margins are being compromised. This would also become part of "corporate sales strategies" that define what the company is all about when it comes to new business, client retention, and new business development initiatives. When companies agree to pricing discounts and less-than-acceptable profit margins, it is typically considered a short-term condition, with hopes of eventual pricing stabilization over time.

Many executives in the New Millennium have claimed that they are working harder for less, meaning that a new phenomenon is in place over recent years, in that clients are squeezing them to work harder for smaller margins. When this situation is real, sales management must work with all other profit and cost centers to bring costs in line with the new overall profit margins. Manufacturing, operational, and customer service efficiencies must be gained to offset lower client pricing. In addition, innovation must be part of the strategy that adds value, allowing profit margins to increase.

Comprehensive sales forecasting, which is what this is all about, then becomes a very critical and high-profile yearly process that can have both short-term and everlasting effects on how a corporation does in any one year or over a defined period of time. Sales forecasting is discussed in more detail in Chapter 9, which the reader is prompted to have reviewed and learned in depth.

Obtaining and maintaining the correct pricing for both you and your customers will make or break the success of both organizations and the relationships that exist between both parties.

Competitive Service and Value-Added Deficits

Complacency is a major killer of many organizations. Just look to the food service, automobile, airline, and travel services industries that all have had many declines in their business profiles over the last 40 years as a result of complacency. The number of players, the number of survivors, and how those companies do business today, as compared to years ago, have all changed dramatically as a result of management complacency. Arrogance, cockiness, and unrealistic self-realizations are all trademarks of complacency.

"We are doing okay, so why change?"
"Why change a successful formula?"
"Things seem to be going okay, I think."
"Sales will get better; they always do!"

These statements are all complacent mindsets that can lead to lack of competitive advantage.

When companies become complacent they tend not to "see the forest for the trees." They get left behind by their competitors who are offering bigger and better competitive services, particularly in the area of value-added capabilities. Companies must be continually reinventing themselves to maintain long-term competitive advantages. This means innovation and value-added and competitive leading-edge initiatives.

Sales managers must be fully and comprehensively aware of three things:

1. What are the changing needs of the customer?
2. What are your competitors doing?
3. What do you need to do to be "state of the art" tomorrow?

The sales manager and organization that has business processes and infrastructure in place to manage those three areas will do well in being competitive in today's ever-changing market place.

In many organizations, this area of concern would fall into the Marketing Department's purview. Irrespective, sales management will always be involved in a big way, as the benefits and consequences will affect sales in a big way. Analysis, fact gathering, and information processing are all things that need to be done by sales managers to determine what you are not doing that is causing sales to slump. This will lead to specific goal revision and tactical changes that will take place to turn around sales that drive better results.

Lack of Qualified Closing Skills

The author believes from his 35-year business tenure that most sales personnel lack "closing skills." They either are afraid to ask for the business or don't know how to, where the result will be beneficial. No matter how good the product or services, closing skills are necessary to finish the job.

The sale is like a baseball game. The opening, the proposal, the product, the service, the reputation, the relationship—all will get you to third base. But to get home, what many consider as the most critical step is the ability to close the deal. The author contends that most salespeople lack this ability to go from third to home. And this means no home run and no sale.

Closing skills are both innate and can be learned. This means that certain people are naturally better closers. They have a "gift" to be able to easily, comfortably, and confidently ask for the order and—the majority of time—get the business.

We know who these salespeople are; we are usually jealous and envious at the same time. We wish we had their persona and gift. But we have alternative options here. Many salespeople can learn the skill set of closing. This is covered in Chapter 9 in more detail.

The important note here is to recognize that, whether innate or learned, closing is an important skill set to hone and master. It will lead to better results.

Poor Proposals from a "Quality Communicative" Benchmark

The author is sometimes agape at what he has seen in the form of written proposals from various companies soliciting his favor. The proposal is what makes an impression. Sometimes it is not even read in any great length or detail, but just its physical appearance will make an indelible mark with the customer that can seriously influence his or her decision making.

The proposal is a communication tool that is supposed to bridge what the client's needs are and how you will fill those needs better then anyone else. It tells the client who you are and what you are about. This is covered in more detail in Chapter 9.

Proposals are often what clients will principally utilize from their RFP/RFQ (Request for Proposal/Quote). It will be the single determining factor in their decision-making process. While we might argue the sense in that, the reality is that we may not be able to control or influence that decision, but must instead learn to navigate successfully through it. Our proposal then must be a quality document with clear, concise communication tools that work, that tell our story, that keep the reader's interest and, ultimately, find favor with the reader.

Lack of Quality Relationship with Buyers

The author has known many sales managers who believe 100% that "relationship" is the single most important factor in the world of selling and buying or Purchasing

Management 101. In many instances this is true. In many instances it is a small part of the ability to earn the business. In either case, it is always a critical factor in most decision-making processes.

Sales managers need to assess the buyer and determine to what extent that "relationship" will be a factor in his or her buying persona. Obviously, if it is a key factor, then one needs to work on that. Finding out what you need to do to further develop that relationship is important.

Many times this might mean social outings: golf, dinner, ball games, with spouses, etc. Many companies have rules about these forms of entertainment, both as sellers and purchasers. You need to know how the playing field operates before proceeding. You do not want to get anyone in trouble or compromise the opportunity due to exorbitant gifts, entertainment, or the like. In the international side of sales, this might have legal consequences stemming from the FCPA (Foreign Corrupt Practices Act), which is covered in Chapter 3. Treading slowly and carefully is usually a good idea on the international side, and this approach works for domestic relationship building as well.

The entire process of relationship building provides several benefits. If clients like you:

- They are more likely to buy from you.
- They are more likely to "work" with you to get the business.
- Price will be less of a factor.
- Communication will be more open and direct.
- There is a better possibility for longer tenured sales and renewals.
- There is a better mitigation opportunity if things go wrong.
- Inside information works to mutual benefit.

Relationship building or relationship management is a discretionary function of sales. It can be the most critical or least critical function. Its importance must be quickly assessed and then acted upon accordingly. As many salespeople will argue: *relationship*. It could be the most important factor in the vendor/client world, and its opportunity could become the destiny of the sale.

Not Selling to the Decision Maker

Too many times we make a great sale story line and presentation—but to the wrong person or persons. We typically find this out when we did not receive the order or business and ask the person we sold to, "Why?" They respond by explaining that the individuals they report to decided to go with another company.

The mistake(s) made:

- Someone else is selling for you.
- You lose control of the situation.
- How are objections and questions being handled?
- What is the agenda of the person advocating on your behalf?
- Is there an "apples to apples" comparison being accomplished?
- Was your best case put forward?

Most of these questions tell the story. Early on in the prospecting time frame, the true decision makers need to be identified. It is this person or persons that you need to meet and work with as to needs and what you have to do to earn the business. This does not mean that you are eliminating the primary contact. It means that you are upwardly expanding the communications to everyone's mutual interest. And when there are obstacles in moving upwardly, that is where you move in, explaining that their company will best be served if you are dialoguing to some extent with the true decision makers.

Your main contact must not feel threatened or concerned about your going up the line. Rather, the contact should be reassured that this will work in his or her best interest too. If you don't "push hard" on this, you may be wasting all your production energies. Getting to the decision makers can be considered as integral a factor in successful sales as the creation of the original opportunity in the first place.

Failure to Convince Prospect to "Buy-In"

You delivered a great proposal to the decision maker. The relationship was there, and you were confident of a sale. But no order is forthcoming. What went wrong?

A lot of things could have gone wrong, with a strong likelihood that you did not convince the buyer you were the best option. Or the prospect simply did not "buy-in" to your story line.

There are a number of possibilities:

- You're not as good as you think.
- The relationship was weak or unfounded.
- You underestimated your competition.
- Price points are too high.
- Proposal was not convincing.
- You sold to what you thought they needed and now find out they needed something else.
- You upset someone in the process.

Regardless of which one of these (or other) factors applies, you need to conduct a postmortem and find out just what happened. You will benefit from the diagnosis on future sales with other accounts. There may also be another opportunity with this client, and you do not want to make the same mistake twice.

Extraneous Issues

Even after a thorough analysis of the situation as to why you did not receive the order, the reason may still be unclear. There are a slew of potential extraneous reasons that may have occurred and that now may have surfaced. These can be even more perplexing and frustrating.

You might find out that your competition is personally related to the buyer. The vendor has a contract in place that has penalties for early withdrawal. Some senior executive up the line wants more bids brought into the RFP equation. Any one of these can cause a "train wreck." They are difficult to anticipate, uncover, or be proactive on. These are the ones that only "experience" will possibly ferret out over time and past occurrences. The point here is just to have an awareness of this potential. Not much can be done about these extraneous issues.

Note that there are additional case studies in the Appendix.

THOUGHTS TO SELL BY...

The Pilgrims made seven times more graves than huts. No Americans have been more impoverished than these who, nevertheless, set aside a day of thanksgiving.

H. U. Westermayer

Chapter 8

The Sales Manager Daily Regimen: Time Management Excelled

It is imperative that the sales manager have a consistent routine each business day that allows for the most effective execution of his or her responsibilities. This will ensure performance for the manager and his or her team—and maximize time management.

Time Management Overview

A person's ability to manage time is based upon his or her ability to manage organization, prioritization, and communication skill sets.

The Visual

A lecturer on time management is holding an empty glass beaker that will hold about a gallon of product. He asks his students, "Is the beaker empty or full?"

They answer, "It is empty." He acknowledges.

He then reaches under his podium and begins to place 1-lb large pieces of rock into the beaker. It takes about 8–10 rocks to get to the point that there is no more room inside the beaker. He asks the students, "Is the beaker *now* full?"

They answer, "Yes?"

He then reaches under the podium and lifts out a bowl of smaller stones, maybe an ounce or two in size, and begins to place the stones between the rocks until there is no more room to fill all the voids, crooks, and crannies. He asks the students, "Is the beaker *now*—really, *now*—full?"

They answer, "Yes?"

He then reaches under the podium and produces a vial of sand and begins to sprinkle the sand between all the little openings between the rocks and stones. He does this for a moment or two until no space is available. He asks the students (who now are very suspicious), "Is the beaker full?"

As reticent as they are, they answer, "Yes?"

He then reaches under the podium and lifts a vase of water, which he begins to slowly pour into the already filled beaker, and to everyone's amazement, the beaker can take on plenty of liquid. After a moment or two, the beaker begins to run over with water. He asks, "Is the beaker *now* full?"

They answer, "Yes," and at this point the lecturer acquiesces and clearly states that the beaker is now full.

The lecturer now makes some points and advises the students of all the things they just learned:

Point 1

A person's capacity to accomplish more is only limited by his or her mindset. The example demonstrated how the students thought the beaker was full at various points, when in fact, there was really plenty of room.

This works in tandem with a person's mental capabilities. We typically emulate that we cannot take on anymore, when in reality, we have plenty of room for more.

Point 2

Our ability to take on more is limited only by how we organize our own beakers. This is true if you believe, as in this example, that your capacity is the internal perimeter of the beaker.

If the person had put the sand in first, would there be room for the stones and rocks? The answer is no.

So how we organize the material into the beaker will significantly affect the volume the beaker can hold.

This compares well to how our brains work. If we organize ourselves in a fashion that fits into our mindset, we then can take on more. Rocks first. Stones second. Sand third. Water last.

Point 3

If we identify the large rocks with the most important things in our lives, such as (but not absolutely for everyone)—our health, our family's well-being, our religious affiliation, our survival, our career, etc.—then we must prioritize these things first.

If we identify the smaller, less important things in our lives, such as (but, again, not absolutely for everyone)—keeping the house clean, taking out the garbage, bringing cupcakes to the office, getting our nails done, etc.—then these activities are prioritized after the bigger, more important things in our lives.

Examples of misplaced priorities:

- How many people might prioritize going to the beauty parlor before setting up a dentist's exam?
- How many people might prioritize going to a professional ball game and then missing their son's soccer team in their final game of the season?
- How many people might get on line for an early morning sale at Home Depot and miss their doctor's appointment?
- How many people might first take care of their car but miss appointments related to their own health?
- How many people might work on a proposal due next week in lieu of attending a 1-day seminar where they will be taught enhanced closing skills?

There are hundreds of examples of people not prioritizing correctly. We know who they are. They are all around us.

- People who "sweat" the small stuff.
- People who get lost in minutia and forget the big picture.
- People who cannot "see the forest through the trees."
- People who continually make poor decisions and prioritize horribly.
- People who are frustrating and disappointing to deal with.
- People who lose sight of what really is important.

The results of these behaviors can be serious. In sales management, they can prevent ultimate success and prohibit achievement. Potential consequences include:

- Stress
- Lost accounts
- Poor use of time
- Not accomplishing the more important things in life and career
- Making lots of people around us upset
- Always being behind in work, being late and not on time, and everything is seriously overdue
- Lots of things are lost, misplaced, or not accessible

Take the Initiative to Change Behavior: It Will Change the Results!

One can achieve successful time management in four steps:

1. Mindset
2. Organization
3. Prioritization
4. Communication

Mindset

One must believe that time management can be achieved and that one can show better results. One must believe that the limits are only defined by his or her mindset.

Even those with various mental handicaps have increased their capacity and have risen to defeat many time-management obstacles.

You must believe in yourself and have the confidence to succeed. Never underestimate the power of positive thinking, the importance of being optimistic (the glass is half full), and the value of having a positive can-do attitude.

This is also a "leadership" skill that will manifest itself to all the people around you and those who follow your lead.

Organization

Practice dictates that we need to organize both our business and personal lives. Later in this chapter, we present a "to do" list, which outlines all the things we have on our plates, both long and short term. This to-do list becomes a photograph of our current and future situation. It then becomes a roadmap telling us what we need to accomplish.

Today, through the use of technology—various hardware devices (BlackBerrys, Palms, etc.) and various software (Microsoft, Apple)—we have lots of tools available to help us create and manage lists of all the responsibilities we have. We can easily stay "connected" to all our responsibilities 24/7 if we structure the right system that works for us.

Prioritization

We need to identify the "large rocks" in our lives. We need to identify the smaller stones and all the peripheral responsibilities, actions, and things in our business and personal lives. We need to list these all out. Use any tool for this list that works for you. Consistency in managing the list is critical to its success.

We need to recognize that this area of prioritization is a *moving target*. It will change hourly, daily, monthly, and over the long term. This means that it must be reviewed on a very frequent basis and updated, tweaked, and modified to meet the needs at that time.

The large rocks on this list are unlikely to change much over time. Health, family, career, children, etc., will always tend to be at the forefront. It is the day-to-day work responsibilities that will tend to change, along with the volume of personal things. You will need to take care of that list of personal tasks right along with all your business items.

Communication

When your day is done, you will probably not get to everything you had listed. This is normal and not an aberration. The key is:

- Getting to the most critical items
- Relisting items and carrying them over to the next day
- Communicating to all those involved

For example, you may have told a colleague that you would get back to him or her by 5 p.m. on a client proposal rewrite. You never got to it. So you now call the colleague and ask if it is okay if you get back to him or her by 9 a.m. the following morning, which turns out to be just fine. The colleague is okay with the new timing because you communicated responsibly and timely.

There are some other responsibilities attached to communicating in regard to time management. These have to do with making sure that your business priorities are aligned with all the interested parties.

For example, the author is now a CEO of an organization in which he has multiple responsibilities. He reports to a Board of Directors. From a common-sense perspective, he needs to make sure that his priorities, particularly those in dealing with CEO management issues, are totally in line with what the board has as its priorities. Clear, concise, and timely communication between all the players is critical here.

And here is another example. Today is Tuesday and a husband wants to prioritize painting the house this weekend. But his wife wants to go visit her sister in another state, with him. The conflict is clear and will cause a problem if not resolved by Friday. He has to communicate timely and responsibly and work out a resolution before the situation gets out of hand.

Both examples emphasize the importance of communicating your priorities to all around you who are interested parties if you wish to mitigate problems and maximize better relationships.

Daily Regimen Planner for the Sales Manager

We recommend that the day be broken down into 12 general subject matters.

- Family
- Physical conditioning
- Mental setup
- Review of long-range goals and strategies
- Review of short-term issues (daily checklist)
- Team contact
- Office contact
- Best use of time
- Lunch
- Afternoon focus
- Summary and setup for the next day and balance of week
- Relaxation

Family

Family comes first. You need to build into your thoughts at the beginning of each day that issues, events, and concerns regarding your family may have to take precedence over various business issues. This is not an absolute, but it must be a conscious thought each morning when you wake up. Prioritize what you need to do each day with a potential family matter at the forefront of concern and possible action. There will be compromises here, but discretion will guide you here, as well.

I meet too many senior executives who, when asked, "What would you do differently?" say that they wished they had spent more time on family issues.

The key is creating a balance. And the balance might be quality of time spent rather then the quantity of time spent.

Physical Conditioning

You need to be in decent shape. You don't need to be "buff," but you need to be height and weight proportionate. You need to be in good general health. The following are some suggested guidelines:

- Eat right and eat healthy.
- Exercise three to four times per week, both cardiovascular and for appearance. As we get older, stretching is very important.
- Get regular checkups.
- Quit smoking.
- Participate in some kind of sports activity.
- Keep the mind active and work on things that promote mental well-being.
- For some, spiritual engagement can also be of value.

A healthy salesperson and manager can accomplish more. He or she will have more energy and be in a better position to raise the bar of performance and meet all the hurdles and challenges one faces in the competitive business climate we are all now working in. Healthy salespeople are better salespeople.

Mental Setup

You need to create an organized mindset. This means getting your priorities in order, which can be accomplished by writing a "to do" list, either manually or electronically. This will itemize all the things you need to take care of, both personally and in business. You should prioritize the list, placing the most important things first.

At the end of the day, you may find that you have not completed every task and item on your list. Hopefully, the most important things were addressed and the balance left for another day, with all uncompleted tasks communicated to all vested parties and relisted.

One must recognize that the to-do list is a work-in-process and is not stagnant but dynamic. It will change throughout the day as issues arise, as problems come to light, and as the forces of business play havoc. So the list must be reviewed throughout the day and updated, tweaked, and adjusted to fit the circumstances of the moment.

Managing this list timely, accurately, and consistently will make or break your sales management prowess.

Review of Long-Range Goals and Strategies

Senior management will set a heading and direction, hopefully with clear-cut goals and objectives. These must be reviewed all the time, and they must be SMART.

SMART
- – Specific
- – Measurable
- – Attainable
- – Relevant
- – Trackable

You must recognize that your daily business regimen will ultimately be guided by these goals and objectives. They set the foundation, direction, and pace of all your efforts, initiatives, and actions.

If you continually ask yourself these questions with respect to the goals you set, you will continually succeed with these goals. The formula does not guarantee success, but it does make goals much easier to achieve.

Review of Short-Term Issues (Daily Checklist and Planner)

We just previously discussed a "to do" list. This list will contain both short-term issues that typically need to be addressed in the "now," but the list must also reflect the longer-term issues, goals, and objectives. The manager can always take action and cause results that work both in the short term and in the long run.

Example 8.1

Tom Cook: Daily Checklist (10/15)
   Yearly Business Goals:
      Increase new business sales by 35%
      Renewal business @ 95%
      Launch the New California Sales Initiative by 11/1
      Promotion and compensation increase by year end
   Personal Goals:
      Get son accepted to Princeton
      Lose 15 pounds
      Lower handicap index to 5.0
      Read two additional novels
      Complete 10th book
   Long-Term To-Do's:
      Rework sales commission program
      Meet with the three largest vendors and clients in the Southeast Sales District
      Organize the sales personnel files and human resource data
      Have all the profit center managers and spouses over to the house for dinner
      Review car allowance program
   To-Do List as of October 15:
      Meet with Jack Carson tomorrow***
      Send the CEO all the sales reports from last quarter, fully analyzed
      Set up Dr's appt for cholesterol check
      Meet with Abby to see how she is progressing with her "to do" list***
      Get car inspected by Friday
      Call other soccer coaches on Bobby's team to see if next Saturday works for the goalie scramble
      Organize the sales meeting agenda for next week***
      Call Sally for her second interview next week
      See John Deloite in the warehouse to discuss the late shipping complaints (include Anne, CS Manager)***
      Arrange tentative agenda for next month's trip to California, Oregon, then onto Japan and China.
   Don't Forget:
      Bob's birthday on Thursday
      Gift for Anne's retirement party on Friday

*** *Must Do*

Team Contact

You have a group of sales executives who report to you. Daily and consistent contact is imperative, and these are best when done in person or in direct conversation. E-mails can be utilized, but only as a last resort. Leaving communications to an "e-mail only" basis is impersonal and does not allow you to interact as successfully as when talking directly. In addition e-mailing does not always show emotion or how a person is really feeling, which might be critical in a given situation.

- Daily contact
- Shows caring and interest
- Demonstrates good business acumen
- Shows that you are on top of what is going on
- Establishes a dialogue wherein you must pass information that gets you involved where you can best assist and create effective support
- Mitigates problems before they become severe
- Promotes a more "securitywise" business practice for those who travel or are out of sight

Office Contact

Whether you travel a lot or are in the office, contact with colleagues and peers is an important element of communicating, socializing, and having effective business relationships.

Meetings on a purely business level are strictly business as usual, but mixing up some business with social activities can also promote camaraderie and internal relationship building. Golf, concerts, games, and other team-building exercises are options.

Office contact needs to be consistent. Long periods of time away take their toll on relationships and people's sensitivities to your value and presence. While we all need to be away on business trips, vacations, etc., these should be kept short, to a week or so, but no longer then two weeks.

For those involved in overseas sales, the length of the trip is always an issue. But if you are in a management role, then the trip needs to be cut to as short as possible.

Best Use of Time

Time management will be a key element of your success in your management role.

We, as human beings, have an unfathomable capability to accomplish, grow, and take more on. For some, this ability is innate; for others, it is learned. Either way, we must acknowledge that we can handle more if we choose to. The key in doing this is how we organize ourselves and how we prioritize all our responsibilities. If we tend to rely on memory, we will be handicapped.

Lunch

Lunchtime can be utilized very successfully for both getting work accomplished and in managing some of the social camaraderie requirements with reports, peers, and senior management. You do not necessarily have to go out. You can order lunch in.

The author often calls a sales meeting at noon. Lunch is brought into the conference room. At these times we often "eat healthy," demonstrating a leadership position. While we eat, we dialogue socially—from ball games, to personal lives, to chit-chatting about coworkers, etc. Allow only 15–20 minutes for this, as the group will tend to chatter for the whole meeting. This "chatter" is important for team building and camaraderie, but it must be kept in check—limited and controlled. During this period, proper decorum in conversation, dialogue, and banter must be maintained. People will tend to get loud and sometimes too funny and even crass. Then we get down to business. In Chapter 9 outlining the best practices of skill sales management, the "how to" of running a meeting is outlined in specific detail.

The meeting time following lunch should be no more than an hour or so, as most people, particularly those with a sales profile, will become antsy, and you are better off allowing them to move on for the day.

Lunches that are held outside the office, particularly those in restaurants, will typically be less formal and more social, as the setting is on neutral ground. In such settings, discussion of serious topics—subject matters with lots of detail and facts and figures—should be very limited and maybe even taboo. It is difficult to lay materials out in a restaurant or work around a waiter's interruptions.

Restaurant meetings are good for laying groundwork, for overviews, and for social discussions. Let the more-comprehensive lingo take place back in the office or in a conference room.

Afternoon Focus

Workers who start early in the day will tend to slow their pace in the afternoon. One reason for having a light or healthy lunch midday is to avoid becoming too docile in the afternoon.

Many sales executives have found that the more serious work needs to be accomplished by noon, and the afternoon is for more-relaxed, less-focused agendas—more strategy, less tactics; more philosophy, less action; more reflection, less conversation. Numerous studies have identified that afternoon meetings are less productive than ones held in the morning.

Sales personnel can also use afternoon time for setting up new business meetings, writing proposals, and communicating with clients and prospects.

Summary and Setup for the Next Day and Balance of Week

It is important that, at the end of each day, the salesperson take time to reflect on his or her "to do" list and activities of that day. Then set up the agenda for the next day. This is a great use of time and will:

- Eliminate responsibilities from falling between the cracks
- Reveal the micro and macro issues in a glance
- Allow for the best use of time
- Combine business and personal "things to do"
- Improve prioritization
- Get more things done

Summary, reflection, and preparation will maximize the opportunity to achieve the best results and one's use of time, both businesswise and personally.

THOUGHTS TO SELL BY...

It takes someone with a vision of the possibilities to attain new levels of experience, someone with the courage to live his dreams.

Les Brown

Chapter 9

Mastering Key Skill Sets

There are a number of skill sets that the successful sales manager must master to rise to the top in his or her field. These are daily achievements that—once brought to high levels of capability—can separate the boys from the men and the girls from the women.

- Forecasting
- Interviewing
- Hiring, firing, and maintaining
- Leading-edge innovation and reinventing
- Confrontational management
- Proposals that work
- Lead development
- Managing the "sales pipeline"
- Running meetings
- Negotiation is key
- Problem solving
- Emotional intelligence

Forecasting

Forecasting is the projection of results into the future for senior management to work with in the planning and staging of the business. Typical forecasting is accomplished year to year but can be taken out 3–5 years and as much as 7–10 years. When done out more than 5 years, this is referred to as strategic forecasting, and is best left to those who are professional, long-term business planners and strategists.

Forecasting is an important skill set for all sales managers. This can be best accomplished by four steps:

1. Information flow
2. Accurate projections
3. Communicating precisely and timely
4. Managing and tweaking the forecast

Information Flow

In order to forecast successfully, sales managers must create a timely flow of data and information into themselves. Quality information is "gold" here and will allow the sales manager the best opportunity of forecasting correctly.

Senior management needs to have quality forecasts, as those projections become the basis for strategic and tactical decision making. Be wrong in forecasting, and you could then be building a house on a weak foundation. It will eventually crumble.

Some of the information we want to obtain:

- Prior company sales results (2–3 years)
- Individual sales personnel results
- Sales personnel circumstances that might affect performance (An example of this might be someone who is retiring in the forecast year.)
- Industry projections
- Global, national, and regional economic indicators and forecasts
- Company forecasting models
- Management goals for forecasting years
- New product and service initiatives coming out of manufacturing, management, R&D, etc.

Accurate Projections

Senior management has to have accurate forecasts. Many sales managers tend to believe that lowering projections may work to their advantage. They do this under the theory that if they end up overachieving, they look like heroes, rather than providing higher expectations that might not be achieved, and then they look foolish.

This is really not the case. Senior management needs accurate information. They are restructuring the company, adding or deleting personnel, adding and changing infrastructure, making IT changes, etc. If forecasts come in too high or two low, then the changes they made, either way, will be too little or too much, and that works against everyone.

If sales management erred to the side of being conservative and sales increased dramatically, then there may not be enough customer service personnel, inventory, or production to satisfy customer needs.

Unsatisfied Customers Are Clearly Not What Anyone Wants

If one made forecasts too high and infrastructure changes were made to handle the increased volumes that did not happen, then allocated monies could be wasted.

Angry Senior Management Is Not to Anyone's Advantage

The best position is to forecast accurately. If you want to hedge a little bit, that can be okay, but it must be at corporate discretionary levels.

Communicating Precisely and Timely

The sales manager must communicate in a number of directions to obtain quality information and interchange with all interested parties. These may include:

- Sales personnel
- Customers
- Vendors and suppliers
- Providers and Channel Partners
- Senior management
- Staff
- Colleagues and other organizational managers

Communications Effect Information Flow for More Responsible Forecasting

The wheels of business forecasting will turn more succinctly when communications are timely and comprehensive. Communicate what you need and do it timely, allowing sufficient and reasonable time for answers and input that is accurate and precise.

Managing and Tweaking the Forecast

Forecasts are at best an art and not a science. It is at best a foreboding into the future. The goal is not 100% accuracy, but 100% effort that will achieve the best opportunities for getting as close to 100%, as possible.

Forecasts are a "static" anticipation of what will happen into the future. Above, we identified several variables that could affect forecasting. Over time, any one of these variables could affect forecasting projections.

The best forecasting models allow room for tweaking to take place as a "dynamic" situation evolves. The economy takes a dive. A key customer announces a significant expansion. A war breaks out. A strike at a plant disrupts the manufacturing process. All are any of numerous situations that could and likely will occur that will impact forecasting models. These likely and anticipated changes have to be structured inputs into the forecasting equation that will allow the forecast to be modified for actual occurrences and circumstances.

Managing the forecasting process takes into consideration any anticipated disruptions that may have occurred from an historical perspective. In addition, looking ahead and asking questions as to what could happen will help in this regard.

Some corporations have risk management or disaster planning as part of their contingency planning process. The sales manager would need to interface with the managers of these initiatives so as to build in any factors, information flow, or data that would be relevant to the sales forecasting model he or she would be developing.

The key to forecasting is to obtain relevant information, anticipate well, and take steps that maximize opportunity.

Interviewing

Interviewing for any personnel position is a critical component of a manager's responsibility. When interviewing for the position of sales, this is a serious task that can make or break your ability to meet your sales goals and projections.

I have learned 10 key steps to take over the last three decades, which I will share with you. These outline a "best practices" approach to interviewing for sales personnel.

1. Know what your needs are.
2. Identify the skill sets of the salesperson against your needs.
3. Turn over all stones both inside and outside of company.
4. Interview as many candidates as possible, following prescreening by Human Resources.
5. Set a time frame for interviewing and a time frame for selection and an anticipated start date.
6. Judge "character" high on the list.
7. Qualify motivational "kick" points, and make sure these are doable.
8. Call referrals.
9. Develop a job profile/description that is very specific.
10. Make sure the offer is contemporary, competitive, with clear and doable incentives.

Know What Your Needs Are

Before hiring, you should make up a job profile that clearly outlines what you are looking for. This needs to be crystal clear and concise. If you need someone who can "close," then state it. If you need someone who has good prospecting skills, then say it. If you need someone who has some very specific technical or engineering expertise, then state it.

Too often, when a hire goes wrong, it is as much the employer's fault as the employee's, because the employer hired without micromanaging the "qualification of the organization's needs process."

Identify the Skill Sets of the Salesperson against Your Needs

This goes hand in hand with the previously made point, with the exception that this best practice requires you to find a person who can meet all or most of the needs that you identified in the profile.

We typically spend a lot of time, resources, and money in training sales personnel. To make a mistake and find out about it months later is disastrous, costly, and very nonproductive. It is best to be diligent in making sure the person you are interviewing can meet the skill sets and qualities that you have needs for.

Take the time to do the interview right. We sometimes are so anxious to fill a spot with a body, and then that is all we have—a body—who can't sell. Takes up space, but can't sell.

Turn Over All Stones Both Inside and Outside of Company

Always look into internal personnel for sales positions. They already know the company, the product, and "how to," and perhaps they have a flair for sales. Plus, you already know their character. In addition, connect all over outside the company— the Internet, newspapers, industry publications, networking, friendly competitors/ vendors/customers, previous employees, etc. Act on all your options in finding good salespeople.

Interview as Many Candidates as Possible, after Being Prescreened by Human Resources

Too often, we are impressed by a candidate and stop the interviewing process. That is a mistake. Now, after 30 years of interviewing, I am "patient" with the decision-making process, and I interview all the candidates. You never know what you might have till you open all the doors. Do not shortchange your best potential option by selecting your first option.

Set a Time Frame for Interviewing and a Time Frame for Selection and an Anticipated Start Date

We generally start the hiring process when we need someone—now. We usually do not have the benefit of a "proactive and advanced" interview process. So we need to set time frames. When would we like the person to start, and what is the "drop dead" date?

This means we have to schedule time for interviewing and a time frame for making a decision. Sometimes, this may mean picking the best candidate, but not necessarily the one who we are most comfortable with. While this is certainly not a preference for hiring, it is a sad reality in normal business practice. Waiting for the "perfect" candidate is a luxury we sometimes cannot afford.

Setting "parameters" of skill sets, dates, and acceptable options is critical to the hiring process when a person needs to be brought on board. One must weigh the risks of not hiring anyone versus the opportunities and risks of hiring someone less than perfect.

Judge "Character" High on the List

The "character" of the individual is high on my list of attributes that I make judgment on. Honest, serious minded, responsible, hard working are some of the character traits I am looking for.

Keep in mind that an important component of how people buy is their confidence in and liking of the salesperson who is selling. The salesperson's "character" determines how he or she is perceived by their prospects and customers and, more times than not, is a significant deciding factor in choosing them as a vendor.

This is an area I do not compromise on. While other "traits" are important—persistence, prospecting process, closing virtues, social talents, etc.—these can be developed and enhanced. Character traits are more innate and tell us more about who the individual is.

Qualify Motivational "Kick" Points, and Make Sure These Are Doable

It is critical to make sure you understand what is available to motivate your new sales hires and that that will work for them. I call these motivational "kick" points.

For example, if a person you are interviewing has indicated that commission compensation and making as much money as possible was important to him or her, then make sure you have a "kick" point or a structure in place that accomplishes the same. If your compensation is based on salary only, then his or her goal would be potentially unavailable unless there is another capability in place.

Another example: a person advises that control over his or her scheduling of appointments and times would be a necessary component of a viable offer. If your company policy is 9–5, with no variances, then his or her concern is an issue.

Call Referrals

I am always amazed how many companies ask for referrals and never call, or only call one or two. You should at least ask for five and call them all. Ask for customer referrals or clients who might be willing to accept a call from a potential new employer. Even ask for clients they lost. They might tell a few things that could have a major bearing on the decision-making and hiring process.

Develop a Job Profile/Description That Is Very Specific

Be very clear in what you put together for a job description, particularly in regard to compensation and incentives. As most salespersons are motivated in part by compensation, a very detailed explanation should be accomplished, with specific examples. If there are milestones for incentives, they should be made clear and concise. If there are travel, social, or peripheral responsibilities, that should also be quantified and outlined.

How prospects will be obtained, along with how referrals will be treated, should also be communicated. Specify the expected work hours and describe the systems that will be used to measure performance. The clearer the offer is, the fewer complications there will be down the road.

Make Sure the Offer Is Contemporary, Competitive, with Clear and Doable Incentives

If you are to attract and hold quality and motivated sales executives, then your offer must be "state of the art" and provide a structure that makes you competitive. The offer must not only be competitive at the time of the offer, but over the course and tenure of employment. Primary compensation, incentives, overrides, bonus schedules, perks, allowances, memberships, etc.—these are all tools that employers can utilize for attracting and maintaining successful and key sales personnel.

Good sales personnel are usually very aware of what competitors are offering, which means that you have to be aware as well. Handle this by being proactive and offering and structuring deals that are ahead of the competition. As a sales manager, you will find the task of developing effective compensation programs to be a major challenge. Think "out of the box" in this regard. Be aggressive, direct, and comprehensive in your approach to identifying what are "market" conditions and how you handle this with each individual salesperson. You will find that each individual will have different motivational triggers, with some wanting money, others influence and power, others security, etc.

Make the time to know what your salespeople need, and then address those needs. You will find this to be highly individual and will require a lot of forward thinking to maintain a balance and fairness to your entire sales team.

Summary in Interviewing

Hiring good salespeople is a critical component of any aggressive organization. Making the wrong hire is not only costly, but can set the company back by months if not longer.

Follow the 10 steps described above. Integrate them into your own style and nuances and you can achieve only success in your interviewing process for sales candidates.

Taking a "best practices" approach to the acquisition of good sales personnel will provide a significant improvement in the hiring process while producing more cost-effective, bottom-line results for you and your organization. Tying character, compensation, structure, motivation, and skill sets into the hiring equation will prove to be a very successful management tool.

Hiring, Firing, and Maintaining

Terminations

The sales manager will often have to terminate sales staff from the organization. Firing is part of the deal. This may come from a previous hire before your tenure or from a mistake you made in the hiring process. Sometimes companies cut back and someone has to be let go. At the end of the day, whatever the reason, terminations are part of the deal in management, no matter how distasteful.

Just keep in mind:

- Follow corporate guidelines, if you have them, in the termination process. Document everything, even if it is "memos to file."
- Be civil and polite. You are dealing with a human being who has feelings. Show respect and dignity throughout the process, irrespective of what the person did or how you actually feel.
- Always try and make the best of a bad situation. Offer encouragement, assistance, and support. Make the termination as "easy" as possible, without bad feelings or sensibilities. Sometimes this is impossible, but you need to give your best shot at making the termination as least painful as possible for both parties.
- Be responsible when coming to the timing, communicating, and executing of the termination action. Be generous in severance packages and how you handle the sales employee throughout the process.
- Be careful of what you communicate to colleagues and other related parties. Many times this can come back to haunt you in the long run.
- Do not burn bridges. In 30 years plus, I have seen relationships go full circle many times.

Hiring

Hiring can be best achieved by following these six steps:

1. Keep a pipeline of candidates available. Always make interviewing and hiring part of your weekly routines, so that when times call for adding sales staff, you are ahead of the curve.
2. Stay close to the competition's sales staff. Know who they are and create the ability to pick up the phone to call them, even if informally.
3. Work closely with your Personnel/Human Resources Manager, who can be very helpful to you when it comes time to hire.
4. In everything you do, make sure you understand that you want to make the place you work attractive to potential employees. Reputation is a key factor here.
5. Make sure your compensation package is both contemporary and competitive—that it is motivating to potential candidates who are looking for chances to earn big money and career opportunities.
6. Engage senior management and encourage them to participate in the hiring process. They can be excellent cheerleaders and advocates for the organization, attracting key sales staff to join.

There are many books and seminars that address the hiring process. Sales managers who have this as part of their primary responsibilities ought to look into these books and participate in such seminars.

Maintaining

A primary responsibility of a sales manager is to maintain the sales staff, kind of keeping a status quo. But for those sales managers who truly want to excel, the status quo is a minimum guideline. The bar must be raised for maintaining sales personnel so that goals can be surpassed and record new business can be achieved.

The task of maintaining the sales staff can be broken down into three areas:

1. Security
2. Career
3. Compensation

A successful sales manager will address all three areas in bringing about the highest levels of personnel maintenance.

Security

Some salespeople need to feel secure in their position and long-term tenure with the company. They want a comfort level, knowing that, if they do what they are required to and achieve planned goals, they will maintain their jobs and be able to make a basic living.

Typical sales personnel are higher achievers than basic salary levels, but in the back of their minds, the security issue is a minimum level of income to pay for food, shelter, and existence. What we are referring to here are some of the basic human needs as identified by the famous Maslow in his theories (Figure 9.1).

Career

The salesperson may want to feel comfortable that there is growth opportunity to go into management, take on more responsibility, and gain greater access to the corporate pie. This growth option may be different for each person, and it is the sales manager's responsibility to sort this out with each salesperson's job description.

It is imperative for each sales manager to understand where his or her sales staff wants to be with respect to their careers and to design motivational incentives for these to be achieved.

Compensation

Compensation is typically a key concern for motivated sales personnel. Compensation programs must be both contemporary and competitive. They must also be designed to keep the salesperson motivated with responsible incentives.

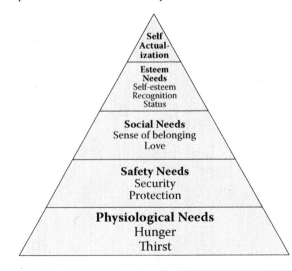

Figure 9.1   Maslow's hierarchy of needs triangle

Most companies pay a base wage and then a commission or override on sales activities upon meeting certain goals. While there are all types of compensation programs out there, the author's experience has demonstrated that the best sales compensation programs are those that provide serious incentives for meeting goals and even more for surpassing them. Compensation programs for sales personnel can be salary, commission, draw, or whatever, but, at the end of the day, it must be based on actual results.

Seasoned sales personnel are always best paid on activity, results, and performance. New sales personnel—to help them get through learning curve periods—may have some base salary, but they need to get into performance-based compensation as soon as possible. This will vary from industry to industry, but from 1 to no more than 3 years would be acceptable in most businesses.

Leading-Edge Innovation and Reinventing

Complacency kills. One must never rely on past successes.

The key skill set to master is to recognize that a company must continually reinvent itself, innovate, and be leading edge in all its strategies and tactics. Sales managers will lead the charge in this regard. "Thinking out of the box" is the everyday "modus operandi" of the successful sales manager. This provides the very best opportunity for all sales initiatives to succeed.

When sales stalled, **McDonald's** reinvented itself by finding new venues to sell in—airports, highways, and overseas markets.

Pepsi created the "Pepsi Generation" that magically caused record sales and growth.

Microsoft is continually progressing into 8.0, 9.0, 9.1 operating platforms.

Audi, a company that was down and out after numerous lawsuits in the early 1990s, innovated a higher end of car design and performance that now has created its own standard in luxury sports and all-wheel-drive vehicles.

TaylorMade Golf is bringing out new drivers—R5, R7, Advanced Burner— several times a year to be cutting edge and enjoys a lead position in PGA player utilization, which allows record sales.

Whirlpool reaches out to customers through an Innovation Process and Design Center that affords the most leading-edge innovations to maintain record sales and growth, here in the United States and in overseas markets.

Many companies have reduced their cycle of innovation to shorter periods of time to stay ahead of the innovation-to-copycatting cycle of foreign competitors.

Once an idea succeeds,

■ Make the most of it.
■ Continually recreate it to make it better.

- Reinvent the idea, again and again.
- If it has a lifespan, go back to the drawing board.
- Bring old ideas back, with a new twist.
- Continually analyze it and make it better.
- Make sure the idea stays contemporary.
- Don't look a gift horse in the mouth; in other words, be thankful for what you have and make the most of it.
- Recognize that success can be fleeting. Take advantage when you can.

Confrontational Management

One of the most difficult issues for people to manage in almost any area of life is how best to "confront" successfully. Most people do not like confrontation. It is threatening and leaves most people uncomfortable. It is not something we typically learn in life, except for a few of us who had platoon sergeants for fathers. Confrontation usually leaves someone upset and angry—and possibly useless.

The art of successful confrontational management is to be able to openly, directly, and freely speak your mind when it is necessary, and being able to make your point without leaving the other party so upset that what you were trying to accomplish gets lost in the emotion of the occurrence. Successful confrontational management leaves the other party with a realistic appraisal of the matter, but gives the other party room to breathe, so he or she will not walk away in such a state that you lose out on what you were looking to accomplish.

You must keep your "eye on the ball" here. The confrontation is not the focus. The focus is that confrontation is just a tool that can be utilized to get you what you need when other options fail.

Making that point—because confrontation carries such a high risk—it should only be utilized as a last option or when other avenues do not exist anymore. Keep that in mind: confrontational management has a certain degree of risk attached to it. One must be careful in moving forward with this option and quickly learn how to master it successfully, because those who use it unsuccessfully become known as bullies, hotheads, difficult, etc., and they can lose their functionality as a manager in the organization.

When you choose to confront:

- Make sure no other options exist.
- Make sure you have all your facts straight.
- Be direct, no-nonsense, and to the point.
- Do not use rhetoric or overly lengthy statements.
- Pick the right time to confront, as doing it at the wrong time can prove to be disastrous.

- Really think out what you are going to say, and try and use words that do not cause the other person anguish or will get them too upset.
- While you need to be direct, you can be direct without necessarily being antagonistic.
- While you may have to end with certain threats or actions, you can end the confrontation on a positive note.

It is important to note that managers who are successful at confrontation have established relationships with their people that allow confrontations to happen. This means that they have gained the respect to have to "rip someone a new asshole" every so often.

Confrontation, when utilized repeatedly, means that you are in the wrong business or are doing something wrong in your management style. It is a tool that should only have to be utilized in particular circumstances on an irregular and infrequent basis.

Sure, if you were a platoon sergeant of new recruits at boot camp, confrontation would be the "modus operandi" for several months and happening all the time. But that is a unique set of circumstances outside the business world. Confrontation in business should not be occurring daily.

Proposals That Work

One of the biggest mistakes a salesperson can make is to give a bad proposal. Every other thing he or she does could be perfect, but if the proposal stinks, then the opportunity will be guided by the weakest link, and the sale won't happen.

The sales manager's role is to make sure that proposals are telling the right story, creating the sale, and providing the venue for the close of the deal in your favor. All written proposals should

- Be concise and to the point
- Minimize rhetoric
- Maximize pertinent information flow of key and central points
- Contain an executive summary
- Be in outline format, with a beginning, a story, and a conclusion
- Recognize that multiple prospect personnel could be reading the material
- Not be too wordy, but make sure everything is explained well (do not leave more questions than answers)
- Provide overwhelming and convincing arguments for choosing you
- Be proactive in identifying strengths and minimizing weaknesses
- Provide closing arguments

Lead Development

Sales managers will gain yards of respect from the sales team when they can provide venues for generating qualified sales leads. This could mean several situations:

1. Creating and allocating specific client leads
2. Finding venues for lead development, e.g., trade shows, telemarketing, etc.
3. Assisting in the finding of lead opportunities
4. Providing direct management support in developing prospect opportunities

In many companies, creating sales leads is left up to the individual salesperson. They are allocated time to accomplish this, and it becomes part of their daily sales activities.

The author has found that this is a typical area that sales personnel struggle in. Sales personnel tend to appreciate organizations that allow the sales manager to offer support in this area.

Remember that sales typically start with leads. So the better quality the start, the more likely is a better finish. Better finishes mean more sales.

In lead development, what can sales managers offer?

■ Managing telemarketing options
■ Finding better lists and prospect databases
■ Finding areas of "centers of influence" where leads can be established
■ Finding networking opportunities for sales personnel to develop opportunities
■ Assist sales personnel in specific lead development tactics
■ Help qualify best lead development options
■ Access technology options that can produce or manage sales leads

The author has found that the more actively involved sales managers become engaged in lead development, the more appreciative sales personnel are and, in the long run, better sales results.

Managing the "Sales Pipeline"

The theory behind the "sales pipeline" is as follows: When you put oil in a pipeline on one end, it will eventually begin to trickle out the other end. After a while, as the oil input increases and the pressure advances, the oil will come bursting out through the other end.

Well, the sales pipeline theory works the same way. In the beginning, sales leads, when developing, will produce a trickle of results at the other end. But as the salesperson fills the pipeline and creates more leads and opportunities, eventually the pipeline will burst through with deals that close.

From a sales management perspective, it is then a responsibility of the sales manager to manage the pipeline. This means that the sales manager must make sure there is a steady flow of leads and opportunities going into the pipeline, so there will eventually be a steady flow of deals that close.

There is another side of this equation. Leads and opportunities that close typically need to be managed, handled, and serviced. This is typically a drain on resources and personnel in operations, manufacturing, logistics, customer service, and possibly finance.

The sales manager then needs to act as a "tender" to the pipeline, making sure that the steady flow of new accounts enters the organization at a "pace" that will service the client responsibly. Too many clients are lost in the opening moments because promises made are not honored, not because of intent but because the company becomes overwhelmed in new business and cannot properly service everyone. Some accounts will then fall through the "cracks." So all the efforts in obtaining the business will be for naught, and no one will be happy about that, particularly a customer.

It is then the responsibility of the sales manager to control the faucet of the pipeline to make sure the volume of new business coming in falls in line with what the company can handle properly and securely. While it sounds great to have record sales, the ability to maintain the business is a major factor here that has a direct influence on the role of the sales manager.

Running Meetings

Eyeball to Eyeball

Meetings that are face-to-face are much more preferable than conference calling. The face-to-face meeting allows both or all parties to see how a person reacts, body language, and more of the emotion/feelings/sensibilities of the situation.

It is typical that sales managers have to run several meetings a week. Here are some pointers in making the most of this time:

1. Have as few meetings, as possible. Too many meetings are time wasters and accomplish little.
2. When you do have to have meetings, set them up early in the day, before 9 a.m., at the lunch hour, or after 4 p.m. The client's time is from 9 a.m. to 5 p.m. Set a policy not to interfere with client time.
3. Set an agenda. Make it clear. Identify what will be accomplished.
4. Set a time frame—when the meeting will start, when it will end—and hold to that.
5. If someone needs to do something at the meeting, or bring a file, etc., then make sure that this is communicated in a timely manner.

6. Control the meeting. Don't allow too much time on rhetoric or on personal or frivolous matters. Keep to the agenda and the points that need to be discussed.

7. Take good notes and write them up for all to see after the meeting ends—no more than 24 hours later, if possible.

8. Agree on action points before the meeting is over. These list what was agreed to, what is left to do by when, and who will do what.

9. Reiterate all points and obtain everyone's acknowledgment and go ahead.

10. Engage the parties to the meeting; get them involved in the meeting agenda, to-do list, or whatever prior to the meeting. It will go a long way in obtaining their quality participation.

11. Then follow up and make sure the meeting was successful and that everything that was agreed to was acted on.

12. Do not feel that all meetings have to bring closure. If the meeting does not bring closure, make sure that the open items are identified and moved forward, as a point of disagreement or contention, that will be dealt with at a later date.

13. Make the meeting and the communications transparent to all parties, present or not, that need to be in the loop. It will be a sign of good faith, leadership, and responsible sales management.

Conference Calling

For conference calling, all of the above meeting points are valid, with the following qualifications:

1. Conference calling is a secondary option to "eyeball to eyeball."

2. Always meet "face to face" on serious matters. Get into a car, train, or plane when you have to.

3. Use Web cams when the technology is available. If you have frequent conference calling with the same personnel, then make the Web-cam capability a definite option. You want to be looking at your audience and participants when you can. The meeting will prove to be of more value when that happens.

4. You may need to talk a little slower or allow a little more time. Clear enunciation of your words is a more critical issue when meetings are not held in person.

5. Make sure everyone is with you before moving on to another subject.

6. Engage the party(s) on the conference line as much as possible to assure that they are paying attention and feel part of the show.

Negotiation Is Key

One of the most important skill sets any manager can obtain and master, and particularly for a sales manager, is that of negotiation. Negotiation is both an art and a science. Giving a proposal to get an order is actually a negotiation. You are negotiating or convincing a client prospect to buy from you. The proposal you give is an instrument of the negotiation process. The science part is more in the strategy of the negotiation. The art part is more in the tactics utilized to bring about the favorable result desired.

Negotiation management can be structured into two areas: strategic and tactical.

Strategic
    Understanding what each side wants
    Obtaining information: mining
    Relationship building
    Developing a strategy
Tactical
    Making the strategy work
    Determining the place, the time, the players
    Executing
    Follow-up

Strategic

This is the philosophy of the deal making. Donald Trump expounds that this is what makes him as successful as he is, and it is probably true to a certain degree.

Abraham Lincoln once said that if he had 9 hours to cut down a tree, he would spend 6 hours on sharpening the axe.

What Lincoln meant was that it was in the preparation of the tools we will use that will get the job done, and that is where we want to focus in order to make things happen the way we want them to.

Many great coaches focus on basic and rudimentary skills—catching, passing, running, shooting, physical conditioning—in order to win. In negotiation, spending time and energy on planning and staging can be critical to obtain your expected outcome. In my many years in sales management, I am always surprised to see a salesperson go into a deal not very well prepared. And then they get upset when the results are not there. One is not going to lose 20 pounds if they are not prepared to sweat.

If we look at the Department of Defense in Washington, DC, and particularly the Pentagon, we see the quintessential strategic center of war. The Pentagon is not tactical at all. The upper-echelon officers in the Pentegon do not go into battle. Instead, they become a centralized point of information flow so they can develop the strategies that lower-echelon officers will follow. These officers then create tactics to win on the ground that the line commanders and soldiers are required to carry out.

When you think of the Pentagon—one of the largest branches of our government—just consider the trillions of dollars they expend to gain information flow, so they can correctly create defensive and offensive strategies to protect our nation. Commercial sales may seem a lot different from military strategy, but in actuality, the concepts are more similar than we probably care to admit. The most glaring similarity is the need to collect information to make better and more-informed decisions. These better decisions will lead to better strategies, which will lead to better sales results.

Understanding What Each Side Wants

In order to understand what each side wants, the negotiator needs to access information, and the more the merrier. The easier side of this equation is to decide what *you* want. This may mean the "order," but it may mean less than that. For example, in the beginning you may be willing just to create an opportunity to quote and not necessarily the order. Maybe in time that will come, but for now, just getting the "foot in the door" is a success all by itself.

Having said that, you must look at the smaller and the larger picture and set goals for just what you want to accomplish. It is perfectly acceptable to have this layered or tiered, meaning that you are okay with various levels of success. For example:

- The opportunity to quote
- An opportunity to test your services
- A partial order
- A commitment to keep you in the proposal loop
- A commitment to use your products or services down the line
- Or even the full and complete order and commitment

Any one of these achievements in the negotiation would be a success. Keep in mind that you are also setting the stage for the future. While the business may not come in today, you will still be here next year when the business does come in.

Your goal setting in the pre-negotiation planning stage must be realistic and attainable. It is okay to set out your goals over time. For now, we are okay with getting the opportunity to quote, but our goal is to eventually get the order and a full commitment within 2–3 years. Strategy is not necessarily "immediate." Strategy can work over the course of time.

Look at the Japanese automakers that now dominate the U.S. auto market. When they first entered the U.S. market in the 1970s, they were losing money and had very small market shares. Their strategy was to slowly increase market share as they went through their learning curves and the U.S. population began to test their cars. Their more methodic and delayed strategy paid off in spades in the long run.

Negotiating with Leverage

The more difficult side may be to determine what your potential prospect or future customer really wants. Too many sales professionals believe they know what the customer wants. They become arrogant and even condescending about that fact.

While it might be true that, by experience, you have a good idea what the client may be looking for, this author adamantly extols that you need to dig deep to find out and make sure you are 100% certain of what the client is looking for.

I have witnessed many sales that go awry because though the proposal may be sound, it is not on target. A rocket launcher or missile may work real well. But if it lands on the wrong bogie or target, even by a few degrees, it is unsuccessful.

The very best of intentions, the very best or proposals will be for naught if they do not address what the customer wants. And I have seen a lot of those. They are typically off target because the salesperson thought that he or she was selling to the customer's needs, and maybe they were, but not necessarily to their wants.

The information-gathering phase of developing the strategy is primarily to determine what the customer wants, expects, and is going to respond favorably to you for. As President Lincoln once said, spend 6 of the 9 hours sharpening the axe. Or in other words, spend a lot of the available time in gaining knowledge, information, and facts that will help you sell what the prospect is looking for, which will significantly increase your odds of sales success and closing the deal.

Example 9.1

You sell life insurance. You have a client, a young couple who you are seeing tonight. You know very little about the couple when you make the call. Your goal is to sell the couple life insurance that evening, as that is how it was were referred to you. By the end of the evening, no sale is made. You will have to make another appointment, if the couple lets you back, to possibly accomplish that.

But done another way, before that evening, you make some inquiries and turn some stones over. You find out that the husband is self-employed and he lost his father 2 years earlier. The couple is expecting its first child at the end of the year. And the couple just bought its first home six months earlier.

Now, when you come to the appointment, you bring some ideas on how the self-employed could obtain the life insurance coverage and have it considered a business and tax deduction. You also will now discuss some mortgage protection products and have brought a few examples. You also have a few products to show regarding combined life and savings products that the couple may be interested with respect to its future newborn. You also found out how the guy's father's life insurance has helped protect his mother's income flow, which you will discuss in detail with respect to what the husband and wife are considering.

When you leave that night you have commitments on a few products and set up a visit for next week to sign papers and pick up a check. You also agreed to meet with the husband's business accountant to work on the tax deductibility portion of his life insurance. Meeting the accountant and making a favorable impression further creates an opportunity with one of his other customers who needs an annuity-type product.

In the second scenario, a "win-win" was established, and the key was quality information prior to the meeting, the negotiation, or the sale.

Being creative and finding unusual and untried solutions can prove to be successful negotiation techniques. Thinking out of the box and bringing surprising solutions can make a big difference in outcomes.

Obtaining Information: Mining

An important concept in information gathering is best described as "mining," meaning the digging down into various layers as necessary to get to the information (to get to the gold or ore or diamonds) that is required for being best informed. You may have to dig down deep. You may have to turn over a lot of stones. You may have to expend time, energy, resources, and monies to secure critical information that will allow you to put together the best strategy to win the negotiation.

Mining is as much an art as it is a science. It takes time, experience, and, as they like to say in the New York market, chutzpah! One needs to ask a lot of questions during mining. It involves exploration and is like being a detective. The quality of the mining will have a lot to do with the quality of the outcome.

Relationship Building

A very important factor in the overall success of business is the relationship that builds between sellers and buyers, the sales and purchasing professionals working in both organizations. I have had many mentors in my sales career who extol that "relationship" is the most important ingredient to the sale.

A bad relationship is certainly a "killer." A good relationship certainly gives advantage. And an excellent relationship will provide the best opportunity to make sure the deal happens to your favor.

Relationship allows trust, friendship, and bonding to take place at the "personal" level. Relationship opens the door for better "mining." People are more likely to "open up" if they trust you. They are more likely to share critical data and relevant facts.

Building a quality relationship takes time and sets the foundation for easier negotiations. It, by itself, is not an "end all," but it is a vital foundation factor for assuring negotiation success. Building relationships is an investment. One would spend time, energy, money, and resources in making sure it happens. Many times, building relationships happens on personal time, weekends, and evenings. This is where "bread is broken," meaning dinner and lunches.

Relationship building shows an interest and a commitment by both parties. It breaks down natural barriers. It opens up more direct and serious communications. It allows for a more "honest" exchange of dialogue. And all of this gives a certain advantage in the negotiation process for both parties, and most certainly the seller.

Some relationship builders include

- Golfing
- Shows
- Dinners at a restaurant
- Dinners at your home
- Doing activities with spouses and families
- Vacation or weekend retreats
- Sporting events
- Hunting
- Gifts
- Hobbies

There are hundreds of options. However, one needs to be careful about the other person's corporate policy in this regard. Many companies have some pretty strict policies for entertainment acceptances. You need to learn about their existence and their restrictions.

Many individuals who are in purchasing or who have buying authority have their own guidelines. In some venues, you have to be careful about the appearance of "bribery" and similar illegal acts. In the Appendix, we talk about the Foreign Corrupt Practices Act, which outlines bribery issues involved with foreign sales and the U.S. government restrictions in this regard.

Once you get past the restrictions and controls, you need to do what is necessary to build a relationship with the buyer. As a sales manager, you will mentor your team in this direction. As a sales manager, you might even participate. However, relationship has costs attached. The sales manager must ensure:

- Internal and client compliance
- Costs are justified
- Return on investment
- Most cost-effective options are utilized
- No extravagance
- Accuracy and no lying, cheating, or stealing or allowing the company to be abused or taken advantage of (This places an onus on the sales manager to preapprove larger expenditures and control expense accounts tightly.)

■ No kickbacks (Kickbacks are illegal and should never be tolerated in sales or utilized as a negotiation tool.)

Relationships are not typically established immediately or overnight. They happen over time. This is important to remember, as relationship building may happen a year before a sale is made. It is part of the sales and negotiation process that, when factored in, may begin to occur years or months before the sale is actually made. It is also an important investment after the sale to maintain the account and even build into it.

Developing a Strategy

You have developed a good relationship. You have relevant information. You have knowledge of what the client is looking for and desires. You are ready to create a "strategy." This is a plan, not an action.

Some sales personnel create a SWOT analysis at this point.

■ Strengths
■ Weaknesses
■ Opportunities
■ Threats

This kind of lays everything out on paper, which allows the strategy to be drawn up. The focus of the strategy is to deal with the weaknesses and threats while keeping the focus on the opportunities and the strengths. The strategic process is one of analysis, discussion, review, debate, and banter. It anticipates eventual action, but it is static in its own right and not dynamic, like the tactics will be.

Strategy is sometimes accomplished by committee or a group format. The sales manager might be the one who engages or manages this process. It is a time for serious and focused thought. You might only get one shot, so it best be thought out well. Allow enough time for this stage.

You need a "devil's advocate" in all strategy debates. This will always provide a varied and challenging perspective that allows better insight to the other side's point of view. Strategy sessions sometimes raise additional questions and the need to fact find some more. The sessions should not be held so close to the actual sale or negotiation that no time will be left for additional review and scrutiny.

All strategies need to be:

■ Simple rather than complicated (Simple is much better than complicated.)
■ Detailed and comprehensive
■ Responsible
■ Ready to be communicated to many levels of recipients
■ Developed with clearly pronounced deliverables

- Proactively dealing with any downside
- Focused to decision-makers' criteria
- Properly timed
- Developed with an action plan and next-step outline

The strategy to conclude a negotiation to your favor is best obtained by structuring on a solid foundation. This foundation is built upon information gathering, mining, building relationships, and making sure you completely understand what the other party wants. They are the keys to developing the mindset on how you plan to succeed—the strategy!

Once the strategy is developed, a plan of action or tactics is the next step that brings you from third base to home.

Tactical

Making the Strategy Work

Now you will see how the strategy comes together and whether it will work. The telling hour is here!

The strategy is the blueprint of the house for the contractor to build. A good blueprint makes it easier for the contractor, but the contractor still has to execute. The execution stage is what tactics are all about. When one is developing the strategy, one must contemplate what tactics are available and which of those might be utilized. Tactics bring the deal to a close and, obviously, a successful close in your favor. This is where the tires hit the ground, where you put the pedal to the metal, where men and women are made, where Action Jackson enters the fray, and where the bell tolls for you.

Example 9.2

A company that sells advertising space to manufacturing companies has a large prospect. A strategy is developed to offer huge magazine space advertisements at discount pricing. The magazine industry is in a downslide, and pricing is a major issue.

The company still needs to get out the "word," but is looking for inexpensive options. The strategy to sell magazine advertisements at discounts is agreed to by the sales team. Now they have to execute.

The tactic is to have the prospect come to their executive conference room, where they will lay out large copy prints showing the ad, the magazine, and the demographics of the audience. The anticipated audience reach and sales will also be outlined near each copy. The retail and the discount price will also be shown, with the savings highlighted.

The boxed text shows the tactics. It addresses the steps taken to deliver the actual strategy to the client prospect. The tactics continue:

The team agrees that it will give the prospect and their advertising committee 20 minutes uninterrupted to review the ads in the conference room. Then they will give a 10-minute presentation highlighting all the advantages, deliverables, and just how the strategy introduced will increase exposure and sales. Then they will have lunch brought in during the discussion phase and bring the meeting to closure by obtaining their feedback and outlining closing statements.

The tactics clearly demonstrate the strategy to enable the negotiator of the sale to bring about favorable closure.

Determining the Place, the Time, the Players

The Place

Determine the place the proposal will be given. This includes the venue. It is typical that proposals be given in writing, but they are often followed up with a visual presentation, often referred to as a "dog and pony show." Where this happens is important to bringing success. In a lot of circumstances you will go to their office, and in many instances this is perfectly acceptable. However, you may want to have them come to your office. When you request this, you are sending out a "scouting party," "a probe," "an inquiry." From their response, you may be able to assess where they are coming from or to what extent they are committed. Many times their interest in coming to your office shows or demonstrates a greater interest in what you have to offer.

Sometimes a neutral setting is more appropriate. A hotel, restaurant, or executive meeting place can work best here. This might work when their office is not the right place and your office may be out of area or not an option.

Among the reasons you may not want to propose in their office:

- They have psychological strength in their domain.
- They are more likely to allow disruptions to occur, breaking up your focus on the presentation or sale.
- The majority of commitment is yours when you are in their office.
- When they come to you, it shows a high interest level.

The Time

The following are some suggestions about the best time to propose and negotiate:

- It is best to propose and negotiate as close to the decision time frame as possible. Do not propose too early.

- Be the last to propose if you have competition. At that point in time, it is likely that they will have a pretty good idea of what they are looking for and will ask better questions and negotiate more openly.
- It is better to negotiate in the morning than in the afternoon. Most studies have shown that executives are more alert and ready to act earlier in the day.

The Players

Probably the number-one cause for failure in proposals and negotiations for business success relates to sales personnel selling to the wrong audience. In the mining phase of strategy, one must absolutely determine the person or persons who are making the decision.

More often than not, our entrée into a business is not necessarily the key decision maker. The initial contact person may be important for opening doors or influencing the decision-making process, but at the end of the day, that person may not be the key decision maker. Many times there may be layers of decision makers, and you will need to work your way up that ladder. This is a process. It may take time, and you will need to exercise patience in this regard.

You must show respect to the person who gets you in the door and the people who move you up the ladder, *but* you must not let them block your access to the decision makers. This is an absolute, and it is potentially a deal breaker. The reason is simple and straightforward. Experienced salespeople will tell you that, in most situations, if you are not accessing the actual decision makers, you are probably wasting your time.

How do you get to the decision makers?

- Ask.
- Ask again until you hear what you need to. Persistence and diligence will pay off here.
- Bring it up, right at the beginning, and make sure everyone understands that, at some point in time, you want access to all those engaged in the decision-making process.
- Structure scenarios where the decision makers must get involved and participate.
- Offer situations where you control the venue and the participants. You must show certain advantages to accomplish this. An example would be to argue that your ability to negotiate the best price and offer will be based upon how their senior management responds to your inquiries and questions directly.
- Sometimes bringing your senior management into the equation will open the door for their senior management to participate and feel better about being there.

Keep in mind that selling and negotiating is a process. The timing of the meetings might be tapered out over time.

- First meeting: mining and probing
- Second meeting: draft-proposal discussion with gatekeepers
- Third meeting: closing the deal with the decision makers
- Fourth meeting: dotting the *i*'s and crossing the *t*'s

The "players" on the client side who are also on your side are critical here. If they can bring in senior management, you may want to do so as well. If the sale is one that is very detailed and product/service-criteria specific, it may pay to bring along an engineer or technician who can better respond to certain inquiries and questions. Inclusion of these people also shows depth and commitment. Of course, you will need to control what these individuals say and do, as they are not sales personnel and could put their foot in their mouth if not watched carefully. That will also depend upon the individuals and their own experiences.

You also need to consider the number of players who will come to the "party." Too many may be overwhelming, while too few may show a sign of weakness. This will be part of the strategic thinking into the tactics of head count at the showdown.

You also need to make sure that you and your negotiators are dressed appropriately for the meeting. Do not under- or overdress. Try and meet the standard offered by your prospect client. Do not assume what they are wearing; ask! And keep in mind that, in many organizations, smart casual is the standard, but sometimes senior management will still be wearing a tie or a dress.

Executing

Show time! I like to look at some of these proposal meetings as another form of entertainment. It relaxes me. And being relaxed is important, as it emulates confidence. Confidence can be contagious and help make the sale. Be too uptight, and that sends the wrong message.

Follow these guidelines in executing:

- Be relaxed.
- Rehearse the material. Know it ice cold.
- Make sure you know all the key mining "finds."
- Emulate being positive.
- Be direct and to the point.
- Answer all the questions and even ask, "Did I answer your question satisfactorily?"
- Make sure one person takes the lead if more than one person is present.
- Do not argue among yourselves. Keep points of contention quiet and discuss later. You can always amend your position.
- Talk to the group, but focus on the decision makers.
- Make it personal when the opportunity opens up.

- Use humor, but with discretion and to a minimum.
- Look into their eyes.
- Ask questions, probe, and mine while you negotiate. That will help you navigate through possible changes and also obtain a feel of where they are at with all that you are delivering.
- Make it a two-way dialogue, allowing them to ask questions, comment, or challenge at any point. This will make the meeting dynamic and more interesting while increasing the opportunity for favorable closure.
- You may not want to close specifically during the presentation, but you can ask some closing questions to obtain an idea where their mindset is. (The Appendix includes a section on closing questions.)

Follow-Up

The negotiation is never really over until all the loose ends are tied up—locked, signed, and delivered. "PO" (Purchase Order) now available!

I have seen a lot of deals go south after a successful close. The details either never got finalized or the process of finalizing the details wrecked the train. Following up and doing this quickly, timely, and responsibly is a necessary component to make the deal close favorably. Sometimes this is where tweaking will take place, and that is okay as long as the tweaking does not nullify what you originally thought you had.

When the last meeting is over, the follow-up should address all the issues that were readdressed before leaving the meeting. It is now time for final closure to move the deal forward into a reality. This is when you can relax and smoke a cigar or do whatever you do to celebrate. *But only when everything is finalized and not before.*

Problem Solving

Part of management's day-to-day responsibilities is dealing with the array of issues, problems, and conflicts that will occur in all the areas of your responsibility. How you handle these and bring successful closure will determine what your peers, subordinates, and senior management think about you. It also makes or breaks the case for advancement. Problem solvers advance firmly and quickly in most organizations.

Senior management develops the image that you are a "can do" person. "Give him or her a problem and watch it get resolved." When management knows that you can handle the daily influx of problems, issues, and conflicts—and do it well—they find significant value in your employment and overall relationship.

Problem solving is discussed in Chapter 7 and in the Appendix. All the examples provide discussion topics and potential resolutions.

While problem solving has some innate qualities, there is some science in its makeup. Here are a few suggestions:

- Do whatever is necessary immediately to stop the bleeding, as a short-term action.
- Evaluate, mine, and collect information as to what happened. At this point, you will probably have to be judgmental. Haste is critical and will show signs of pomposity and arrogance to some extent, but that may be necessary in a difficult scenario where you have to collect information, where people are tentative, and where time is running out.
- Bring the affected parties together and ask them for a solution. This helps mentor and train. Discuss their perspectives and offer your solution. Then come to an agreement and act.
- Sometimes the first meeting may not bring immediate resolve but only serve to frame the issues at hand. And that is okay, as you do not need to feel the necessity to bring immediate resolution if you have some additional time. Patience is a real virtue here when it can be exercised.
- Take action on the solution. Test and make sure it is working. Tweak, if necessary.
- It is important to follow up in a timely fashion to make sure your action is working. If not, go back again and re-do until you have a solution at hand.

Emotional Intelligence

Emotional intelligence (emotional quotient, EQ) is a relatively new discussion point in corporate America coming from a group of progressive corporate cultural icons who have studied the subject in great depth. Some attribute the discussion to Adele Lynn, Robert Cooper, Ayman Sawaf, Bob Kelly, and Dan Coleman. They all identify EQ as the dimension of intelligence responsible for our ability to manage ourselves and our relationships with others.

EQ is the distinguishing factor that determines whether we make lemonade when life hands us lemons, or whether we spend our life in bitterness. EQ is the distinguishing factor that enables us to have wholesome, warm relationships or cold, distant ones. EQ is the distinguishing factor between finding and living our lives' passions or just existing.

In the business world, I believe that EQ is the major factor of differentiation between mediocre managers and leaders and great ones. In the business world, however, so much of our emphasis has been placed on intellect. It has all been on IQ and the analytical, factual, and measured reasoning power that IQ represents. Make no mistake; intellect has proven invaluable to drive success in business and life. Financial decisions based on analytical details, sound strategies based on facts and data, and processes and procedures based on review and analysis are all critically important.

To get to the next level of business, we combine IQ and EQ to raise the bar of all our skill sets and merge them into a persona and actions that exude confidence and prowess, causing our own inspiration as well as providing a reason for others to follow.

In life, IQ would be akin to the athlete who practices all the time, is in the best shape and physical condition, continually studies all the plays, but is time and time again unable to deliver wins. It is also the actor who can sing, dance, and act, who works real hard and knows all the lines, but is never pursued by the directors as he or she totally lacks "stage presence." It is also the beautiful woman who has the looks, the figure, the intelligence, all the perceived talent, and who is constantly being pursued, but who has difficulty in relationships and goes through life alone. It is also the businessman whose father started the business, who has all the schooling, the training, and did all the right things, but who can never rise to his father's place.

In all these examples, the formula for success was there, but it just did not happen. We all know numerous situations like this in our business and personal lives. They all seem to get to "third base" but cannot get "home." And even in our own circumstances, we have probably had times when we felt like these examples. Some use the phrase, "not seeing the forest through the trees"; or "the ship has sailed, but it does not know where it is going"; or "there are many animals to herd, but no pastures to show them."

In business I have found that these people lose out because they are unable to connect the dots. They have good intentions, all the fundamentals, but lack the ability to make it all bear fruit.

Consider the case of a very intelligent CEO from an Ivy League school. He has 20 years of training, worked his way up the ladder, has always been successful. He seems to go through life and business without a care—kind of the golden child. He finally has his first major challenge, where all can be won or lost, and he loses. He is unable to muster the troops and lead the team through turbulent waters or navigate them to resolution. It seems he has all the talents, but is unable to bring it all together and make it happen.

Most highly regarded leaders have EQ. They are commanding, intelligent, intuitive, and most of all can get others to follow. Few people have all the skill sets and a high degree of EQ.

As this concept of EQ develops into more of a science and its traits and characteristics are identified, sales managers will look to raise the bar of their capabilities and, ultimately, their performance.

Some EQ considerations:

■ Understanding that the job is not just thinking and doing, but to get others to think and do

- Seeing yourself realistically and getting others to be more honest with themselves and with the world
- Getting others to be their very best
- Learning the relationship between thinking and acting, imagining and creating, believing and living
- Recognizing that everything is connected directly and indirectly
- Being able to connect the dots to conclusion, and remembering that everything eventually needs closure and that the timing of this is critical
- Understanding that articulation often separates the good from the best
- Recognizing that perception is very often reality, and knowing when it is not
- Learning how and why people behave the way they do; studying human nature
- Seeing the big picture and also paying attention to vital details
- Learning to focus
- Recognizing that health is everything—physical and emotional
- Learning to command, yet be respectful
- Listening well
- Understanding that business is business and that personal is personal; learning to know when they are the same and when they are different
- Being street smart
- Recognizing when to be patient and when not to be
- Being more responsible, less fair
- Showing common sense, intuition, a realistic perspective, and a forthright demeanor, all of which are virtues
- Being honest, considerate, direct, and no-nonsense
- Being traditional, contemporary, and futuristic
- Always influencing in a positive way
- Realizing that stimuli influence mindset (beliefs), which causes thoughts, which influences behavior, which causes actions that influence results (We generally choose our stimuli, the beginning of how we perceive and, ultimately, influence the world.)
- Not sweating the small stuff
- Approaching every day with a positive can-do mindset
- Compromising everything, except your values
- Creating "win-win" scenarios
- Reducing your emotional highs and lows to more of a steady demeanor
- Taking well-thought-out risks
- Knowing when to exercise passion, and compassion
- Knowing when to delegate, mentor, and lead
- Always being grateful and living every moment and day as a gift

There has been both a seasoned and recent debate whether all these considerations are innate or whether they can be learned. For sure, they can be learned to some extent. For those who have the benefit of these innate gifts, they can certainly be enhanced and bettered.

To some, many of these EQ skills come naturally. For others, they have to be learned, practiced, and highlighted in everyday consciousness and action. For these EQ skills to work in building the character of a person, they must be practiced consistently and in all aspects of a person's business behavior and life persona.

The listed EQ considerations, when practiced with all the skill sets outlined in this book, will create a formula that will maximize your opportunities for ultimate success in sales, sales management, and in life.

THOUGHTS TO SELL BY...

Gratitude unlocks the fullness of life. It turns what we have into enough, and more. It turns denial into acceptance, chaos to order, confusion to clarity. It can turn a meal into a feast, a house into a home, a stranger into a friend.

Melody Beattie

Chapter 10

Best Practices: Sales Management Excellence

We have outlined 10 steps for the sales manager to build into his or her personal practice to obtain the best performance and establish long-term consistent results.

1. Health
2. Remember who you are and where you came from
3. Be consistent
4. Raise the bar for yourself
5. Raise the bar for your team
6. Maintain a mindset of improvement and maintain the learning process
7. Manage locally; think globally
8. Be altruistic
9. Always lead and set a positive example
10. Always take the high road

Health

You must maintain good physical and mental health. It will make you more productive. It is a good leadership quality and allows you to both function well and look your best.

If you are going to lead a group of individuals whose presentation and persona make a difference on how they are viewed by prospects and clients, then you need to look your best and have a quality appearance.

A healthy mind works more effectively. It is more responsive and it can handle stress better.

From a time-management perspective, you need to build in time for:

- Regular doctor, dentist, and other medical professionals appointments
- A regular exercise regime
- Mind and spiritual retreats and exercises
- Quality time for yourself, family, and friends
- Activities to reduce tension and stress
- Eating a healthier diet
- At least 5-7 hours of "sound/deep" sleep each night
- Helping others and volunteering, which will also help you feel better

Remember that appearance is part of selling and management, and your health affects appearance.

Remember Who You Are and Where You Came From

Those who are reading this are probably already successful, to some extent, or will be there shortly.

Never forget from where you came. Success can breed contempt, impatience, and arrogance. This will destroy relationships and make you less effective as a manager and certainly as a leader.

Remembering what it was like to be struggling, a rookie, or a new salesperson—all of these feelings will help in developing compassion and understanding. It will allow you to be tolerant and patient and more thoughtful.

You probably had a time early on that you had doubts, concerns, and were insecure. Well, now others with less experience will look to you to carry them through.

Remembering who you were and where you came from will go a long way in earning respect and therefore the confidence and trust of your peers and your sales staff.

Be Consistent

Consistency is important. Just think about the person who wants to lose weight and begins a diet. He or she eats correctly on Monday and Tuesday, but binges on Wednesday; eats well on Thursday, but binges on Friday. The diet will not work because there is no consistency of action. As a matter of fact, the diet days are a waste of time because the binging will negate most of their positive effects. It could even be more harmful in the long run.

How about the person who is going to tone up by exercise. He or she enters an exercise regime on Monday, but allows six days to pass before exercising again.

Then exercises next Tuesday and allows five days to pass before exercising again. There will be no "toning," as the exercise regimen lacks any degree of consistency.

What one does that works will only work in the long term if it is done consistently. This requires determination, perseverance, and grit. Most people have goals, dreams, and ideals. Only those with the discipline of consistent behavior will make them happen.

Closing the gap of wanting to and doing is a great chasm, only navigated by a few. If you truly want to successfully manage, then you must make consistency a strong character trait.

Raise the Bar for Yourself

Do not settle and compromise what you can accomplish. Your limitations are only set by what you believe in. If you develop a mindset that you can accomplish your dreams, then you will.

Being successful is taking gradual steps. Hopefully most are forward, but some will even be back. There will be times that to move ahead you will have to take two steps backward.

You must continually "raise the bar" of expectations for yourself. Do not allow complacency to set into your behavior. Continually strive to be the best and to do better. This is also a leadership issue, as others will be watching and following you. How can you expect others to keep reaching higher when they don't see you doing it? It is a funny thing about leadership. It takes leadership!

Leading by example will get others to exercise the quality traits that will allow them to continually strive harder and further. This is also an example of the inspiration offered by a coach in a sporting event, such as discussed in Chapter 1.

Raise the Bar for Your Team

Now that you have raised the bar for yourself, you can raise the bar for your team. This can be accomplished both on a team basis and by each person individually. This is setting team and personal goals that make everyone reach higher and achieve even more then they all felt possible.

If you have done a good job at "raising your own bar," then you have demonstrated to all those reporting in to you that they too can succeed and can accomplish more than expected. They can "raise their bar" too and, following your lead, succeed!

When approaching the team as a group, you are looking at a more generalized picture of what they all need to accomplish a higher set of achievements. But when "raising the bar" for the individual, a lot more thought and consideration has to go into the process. You are now dealing with an individual with a unique set of traits, capabilities, and fears. Certain fears can be laid aside in a group initiative, but when asked to be accomplished individually, fear can be a devastating adversary to succeeding.

The higher goals for individuals must be carefully structured and executed. For some individual sales personnel, an aggressive approach is warranted. For others, a more conservative, possibly progressive approach be accomplished.

Flexibility needs to be part of the "raising of the bar" to allow for uncertainties and potential problems that might arise, both on a team and an individual basis. Having Plan B's in place is not a bad thing.

Maintain a Mindset of Improvement and Maintain the Learning Process

Complacency is a very negative attitude in anything we manage, but even more so in sales and sales management responsibilities. If one is not moving ahead, then one is either staying still or moving backward. Both of those are killers. The author calls them both "complacency."

Complacency kills. One needs to counter this mindset by continually getting better and improving. Some considerations:

- Recognize the importance of saying and maintaining that you can always get better.
- Take formal classes. Get your degree, your MBA, or professional certifications.
- Take in information from numerous resources—the Internet, TV, print media (magazine, journals, and newsletters)—on a consistent basis. This includes information not only related to your job, but information that makes you more informed on a variety of subjects to help round you out as a classy, worldly, intelligent, and informed person.
- Attend seminars, conferences, and trade shows.

You must never develop the mindset, irrespective of your level of success, that you know it all or have nothing left to learn. There is always room for improvement, betterment, and becoming an improved salesperson, manager, friend, spouse, or whatever.

Manage Locally, Think Globally

When it comes to sales and business development, managers must operate on a local basis, but they need to think on a grander scale: on a global scale. Sales personnel and the management of that team are on a local level. But what they do, where they do it, and how they go about their business development must look at a grander picture, which is the world.

Foreign sales initiatives, global markets, and worldwide campaigns are state-of-the-art. Thinking strategically and opening efforts into the global markets creates additional opportunity and is critical for long-term survival. Sales team tactics may be operated here in the United States on a local basis, but the strategies for higher levels of success must be accomplished through broader avenues.

The successful sales manager of the new millennium is truly global in his or her thought process, the strategies to execute, and the activities to make it all happen. Leadership and insight into this larger picture is absolutely imperative for the sales manager wanting to reach the top.

Be Altruistic

Altruism: "uncalculated consideration of, regard for, or devotion to others' interests."

Webster's 2002

Or, in other words, altruism means to give of oneself, unselfishly, to the greater good of mankind. This is a quality trait for everyone, but particularly for those in managerial and leadership positions, and even more so for those in sales management.

Sales, by its sheer sense, has a very selfish component to it. Many nonsales personnel believe that only selfish people work in sales, so all salespeople must be selfish. We know that not to be necessarily true across the board. While there are some selfish components to sales, most mature salespeople grow out of that state and become more well-rounded in character traits that are less selfish.

The author strongly believes that sales managers need to take on activities and responsibilities that accent the "giving side" of their personalities and demeanors. They can do this by becoming involved in religious, social, and local organizations that regularly take on activities that "give back" to society. Charitable, philanthropic, and benevolent organizations are excellent options. Participation in such activities will show another side of the sales manager that demonstrates leadership through altruism.

One can never "stoop so low, as to help another." The more one gives, the more one gets.

Always Lead and Set a Positive Example

Managers are people who are looked up to, like a mother, father, big brother or sister, rabbi or preacher, professional athlete, military general, etc. You need to be conscious of this fact and act and respond accordingly.

Setting a good example, all the time, is a critical factor in having people follow you. Setting a positive circumstance, upbeat, can-do, winning approach consistently is a behavior that will rub off on the people who work for you.

Sales personnel are always facing difficult odds—placing a dependency on the manager they report to—to always be positive and see the glass as half full. You must always be realistic, but always upbeat.

Excellent sales managers lead by setting a positive example. This means that sales managers must always think about what they say and do—before saying and doing—and then bring into the statement or action a course of positive and forthright direction. High and positive energy is a behavior pattern for sales managers leading a team of sales professionals. In some industries and organizations, sales could be considered the most difficult part of the job.

Constant challenges, negative buyers, frequent rejections are all part of the sales process. The sales manager must assist the sales team in overcoming these barriers, and has the best chance at doing so by remaining positive and upbeat.

Even when you are feeling low yourself, for any number of reasons, you must rise above those negative feelings and always emulate positive energy. The sales manager must learn to focus away from things that bring his or her team's feelings down and remain focused only on those things that offer hope, promise, and success.

Always Take the High Road

Management means we have options. Many times, choosing the right option is not clear. It is not black and white, but gray. Many times, making the right choice is not easy and presents a double-edged sword when we weigh the consequences of our choices. Many times the choices will force solutions that are dubious and uncertain.

It is at those times that the author sets as his benchmark the option that "takes the high road"—the choice that is morally, ethically, and socially correct. And that choice may ultimately be incorrect, from a bottom-line results-driven benchmark. But when the direction is uncertain, taking this high road can never be too far off from the right action.

THOUGHTS TO SELL BY...

The vitality of thought is in adventure. Ideas won't keep. Something must be done about them.

Alfred North Whitehead

Chapter 11

Transitioning from Sales to Sales Management

Why are you now in management?
Dealing with colleagues and peers
Being of value
Be a "turtle"

Some questions and thoughts about the sales management transition, which will be reviewed in this chapter.

Why Are You Now in Management?

Many sales managers ascended to that position because they were good in sales. That can be a critical error, as being good in sales does not necessarily mean being good in management. Actually, it can be a recipe for a disaster. Management requires a greater array of skill sets and talents that go way beyond just being good in sales. All of those skill sets have been outlined in the book in all the preceding chapters and in the Appendix.

Sales management and management in general requires a much more serious level of commitment, sacrifice, and dedication to time, people, and the company.

Your opportunity in management may have come from any one of the following circumstances:

- You are a top-notch salesperson.
- You have expressed an opportunity to move on in your career.
- You believe this is an avenue for making more money.
- Management believes that you are the person for the job.
- You earned the right for the opportunity.
- You're the last person standing (i.e., nobody else wants the job).

It is important to gain insight for the reason for your transition to management, because it will make a difference in how you move ahead and what you will have as expectations and time frames for succeeding. It is also important in your dealing with your senior management and what they have as goals and expectations—and the timing of same.

For example, if you lack management prowess and are just a good/great salesperson, then your focus would be on management issues. If you demonstrated some management prowess and that is what moved you into this position, you may end up moving faster in taking charge rather then needing more time.

Regardless of the reason, you are now in a position where you have to perform. All the points and references in this book will assist you in becoming a good manager. Do not forget from where you came as you rise up the ladder. Arrogance and condescension are killers, and you will lose the respect of everyone who has to deal with you, particularly those who report to you.

Keeping centered, focused, and with an eye on the ball will be key factors in your transition progress. This progress takes time, and it is okay to set goals that reach out over several months to a year for you to fully take over and, more importantly, succeed.

Dealing with Colleagues and Peers

One of the more challenging obstacles you will face when you move from sales into sales management is how to handle all the personal relationships with the peers, friends, and colleagues you have left behind. This will be a delicate issue, and in most cases, no matter what you do, not everyone will be happy.

First, you need to change your mindset in dealing with friends. When you accepted the position, you potentially left those friends behind or minimally changed the nature of your relationship forever. If you are not prepared to allow that to happen

Being of Value

One goal that you should have that will help you to quickly earn respect from all those around you is to be of value to everyone.

What do we mean by that statement? You earn respect by accomplishing. When you accomplish things for others and they are impressed and comfortable with your performance, that creates the atmosphere for gaining respect. Once respect is gained, the doors open for other beneficial relationships: people will follow you more, listen to you better, and do what you need them to.

Example 10.1

Senior management needs you to deal with a client problem. You jump on this and take care of it. You surpass their expectations, and additional business comes out of the matter. Respect is beginning to be earned.

Your counterpart in finance has a collection problem and needs you to get involved. You make a visit to the client, along with the salesperson, and resolve the issue. Finance is happy and appreciates your involvement, bringing this to a favorable close. You are earning their respect.

The shipping manager is having difficulty making deliveries to a new account, and the salesperson seems not to take interest. The shipping manager asks for your assistance. You set up a conference call with the salesperson and the client. You find out that the labeling requirements are not being done correctly; and that is why the deliveries are not being made. You work out a solution with shipping and the client. The next and the following shipments all run a lot more smoothly.

You have gained the respect of the shipping manager, the salesperson, and the client's receiving manager.

In all three examples, you were of value to all the people who you interface with. When that happens, you earn respect. The rewards of respect come in spades. Those spades offer all sorts of leadership and management benefits that will make the overall sales management responsibilities go smoother and allow you to be more effective. As a new sales manager, you need to think about the tasks, assignments, and problem-solving techniques that will win the respect of your team.

Be a "Turtle"

Being a turtle has two meanings: winning the race and taking risk. For new sales managers who are anxious to succeed, be wary of being the rabbit out of the starting gate.

The Appendix of this book includes a whole workshop presentation on sales management for first-time sales managers.

THOUGHTS TO SELL BY...

You can have brilliant ideas, but if you can't get them across, your ideas won't get you anywhere.

Lee Iacocca

Concluding Remarks

There are a lot of things we must now consider in becoming first-class salesmen and sales managers. The road to high achievement is not an easy one. Those who are committed and willing to make the sacrifices and compromises outlined in this book on a consistent basis will then have a proven formula that will allow them to increase their sales and become successful sales managers.

There is no secret formula, but there are things we need to know and things we need to act on—all of which lie within this book's chapters and expansive appendix. Make the time to read. Make the commitment to learn. Take the initiative to make things happen. The results are there to be had. The bar can be raised and lifted highly.

Skill sets, information flow, action plans, quality communications, and lead generation are all the tools necessary to move mediocre sales management into great sales management. The information on all these subjects and much more has been outlined, detailed, and delivered to the reader in an easy-to-understand approach.

Success is what it is all about. Read this book and practice its teachings, and you shall go forward with the best opportunity to succeed.

THOUGHTS TO SELL BY...

In sales, do not focus on "results" ... but focus on all the energy, the strategies and the actions that create the opportunities ... and the sales will most certainly follow.

Thomas A. Cook

Appendix

Recommended Books on Foreign Cultures
Recommended Banks Managing Currency Risks
Recommended Schools and Programs for Sales Management Training
Foreign Corrupt Practices Act (FCPA): Department of Justice Extract
Political Risk Overview
Global Risk Management
Information and Technology in Sales Management
"Making Someone Sell" article
Sales Management Seminar: Newly Appointed Sales Manager Workshop Agenda
Negotiation: Best Practices Outline
Closing Questions
Presentation for First-Time Sales Managers
Sales Management Case Studies Workshop
What International Salesmen and Travelers Need to Know about U.S. Customs (CBP)

Foreign Corrupt Practices Act (FCPA): Department of Justice Extract

United States Department of Justice
 Fraud Section, Criminal Division
 10th & Constitution Avenue, NW
 Bond Building
 Washington, D.C. 20530
 phone: (202) 514-7023
 fax: (202) 514-7021
 internet: www.usdoj.gov/criminal/fraud/fcpa/fcpa.html
 email: FCPA.fraud@usdoj.gov

United States Department of Commerce
Office of the Chief Counsel for International Commerce
14th Street and Constitution Avenue, NW
Room 5882
Washington, D.C. 20230
phone: (202) 482-0937
fax: (202) 482-4076
internet: www.ita.doc.gov/legal

Introduction

The 1988 Trade Act directed the Attorney General to provide guidance concerning the Department of Justice's enforcement policy with respect to the Foreign Corrupt Practices Act of 1977 ("FCPA"), 15 U.S.C. §§ 78dd-1, *et seq.*, to potential exporters and small businesses that are unable to obtain specialized counsel on issues related to the FCPA. The guidance is limited to responses to requests under the Department of Justice's Foreign Corrupt Practices Act Opinion Procedure [described under the heading "Guidance from the Government"] and to general explanations of compliance responsibilities and potential liabilities under the FCPA. This brochure constitutes the Department of Justice's general explanation of the FCPA.

U.S. firms seeking to do business in foreign markets must be familiar with the FCPA. In general, the FCPA prohibits corrupt payments to foreign officials for the purpose of obtaining or keeping business. The Department of Justice is the chief enforcement agency, with a coordinate role played by the Securities and Exchange Commission (SEC). The Office of General Counsel of the Department of Commerce also answers general questions from U.S. exporters concerning the FCPA's basic requirements and constraints.

This brochure is intended to provide a general description of the FCPA and is not intended to substitute for the advice of private counsel on specific issues related to the FCPA. Moreover, material in this brochure is not intended to set forth the present enforcement intentions of the Department of Justice or the SEC with respect to particular fact situations.

Background

As a result of SEC investigations in the mid-1970s, over 400 U.S. companies admitted making questionable or illegal payments in excess of $300 million to foreign government officials, politicians, and political parties. The abuses ran the gamut from bribery of high foreign officials to secure some type of favorable action by a foreign government to so-called facilitating payments that allegedly were made to ensure that government functionaries discharged certain ministerial or clerical duties. Congress enacted the FCPA to bring a halt to the bribery of foreign officials and to restore public confidence in the integrity of the American business system.

The FCPA was intended to have and has had an enormous impact on the way American firms do business. Several firms that paid bribes to foreign officials have been the subject of criminal and civil enforcement actions, resulting in large fines and suspension and debarment from federal procurement contracting, and their employees and officers have gone to jail. To avoid such consequences, many firms have implemented detailed compliance programs intended to prevent and to detect any improper payments by employees and agents.

Following the passage of the FCPA, the Congress became concerned that American companies were operating at a disadvantage compared to foreign companies who routinely paid bribes and, in some countries, were permitted to deduct the cost of such bribes as business expenses on their taxes. Accordingly, in 1988, the Congress directed the Executive Branch to commence negotiations in the Organization of Economic Cooperation and Development (OECD) to obtain the agreement of the United States' major trading partners to enact legislation similar to the FCPA. In 1997, almost ten years later, the United States and thirty-three other countries signed the OECD Convention on Combating Bribery of Foreign Public Officials in International Business Transactions. The United States ratified this Convention and enacted implementing legislation in 1998. See Convention and Commentaries on the DOJ web site.

The antibribery provisions of the FCPA make it unlawful for a U.S. person, and certain foreign issuers of securities, to make a corrupt payment to a foreign official for the purpose of obtaining or retaining business for or with, or directing business to, any person. Since 1998, they also apply to foreign firms and persons who take any act in furtherance of such a corrupt payment while in the United States.

The FCPA also requires companies whose securities are listed in the United States to meet its accounting provisions. See 15 U.S.C. § 78m. These accounting provisions, which were designed to operate in tandem with the antibribery provisions of the FCPA, require corporations covered by the provisions to make and keep books and records that accurately and fairly reflect the transactions of the corporation and to devise and maintain an adequate system of internal accounting controls. This brochure discusses only the antibribery provisions.

Enforcement

The Department of Justice is responsible for all criminal enforcement and for civil enforcement of the antibribery provisions with respect to domestic concerns and foreign companies and nationals. The SEC is responsible for civil enforcement of the antibribery provisions with respect to issuers.

Antibribery Provisions

Basic Prohibition

The FCPA makes it unlawful to bribe foreign government officials to obtain or retain business. With respect to the basic prohibition, there are five elements that must be met to constitute a violation of the Act:

A. Who

The FCPA potentially applies to *any* individual, firm, officer, director, employee, or agent of a firm and any stockholder acting on behalf of a firm. Individuals and firms may also be penalized if they order, authorize, or assist someone else to violate the antibribery provisions or if they conspire to violate those provisions.

Under the FCPA, U.S. jurisdiction over corrupt payments to foreign officials depends upon whether the violator is an "issuer," a "domestic concern," or a foreign national or business.

An "issuer" is a corporation that has issued securities that have been registered in the United States or who is required to file periodic reports with the SEC. A "domestic concern" is any individual who is a citizen, national, or resident of the United States, or any corporation, partnership, association, joint-stock company, business trust, unincorporated organization, or sole proprietorship which has its principal place of business in the United States, or which is organized under the laws of a State of the United States, or a territory, possession, or commonwealth of the United States.

Issuers and domestic concerns may be held liable under the FCPA under *either* territorial or nationality jurisdiction principles. For acts taken within the territory of the United States, issuers and domestic concerns are liable if they take an act in furtherance of a corrupt payment to a foreign official using the U.S. mails or other means or instrumentalities of interstate commerce. Such means or instrumentalities include telephone calls, facsimile transmissions, wire transfers, and interstate or international travel. In addition, issuers and domestic concerns may be held liable for any act in furtherance of a corrupt payment taken *outside* the United States. Thus, a U.S. company or national may be held liable for a corrupt payment authorized by employees or agents operating entirely outside the United States, using money from foreign bank accounts, and without any involvement by personnel located within the United States.

Prior to 1998, foreign companies, with the exception of those who qualified as "issuers," and foreign nationals were not covered by the FCPA. The 1998 amendments expanded the FCPA to assert territorial jurisdiction over foreign companies and nationals. A foreign company or person is now subject to the FCPA if it causes, directly or through agents, an act in furtherance of the corrupt payment to take place within the territory of the United States. There is, however, no requirement that such act make use of the U.S. mails or other means or instrumentalities of interstate commerce.

Finally, U.S. parent corporations may be held liable for the acts of foreign subsidiaries where they authorized, directed, or controlled the activity in question, as can U.S. citizens or residents, themselves "domestic concerns," who were employed by or acting on behalf of such foreign-incorporated subsidiaries.

B. Corrupt Intent

The person making or authorizing the payment must have a corrupt intent, and the payment must be intended to induce the recipient to misuse his official position to direct business wrongfully to the payer or to any other person. You should note that the FCPA does not require that a corrupt act *succeed* in its purpose. The *offer* or *promise* of a corrupt payment can constitute a violation of the statute. The FCPA prohibits any corrupt payment intended to *influence* any act or decision of a foreign official in his or her official capacity, to induce the official to do or omit to do any act in violation of his or her lawful duty, to *obtain* any improper advantage, or to *induce* a foreign official to use his or her influence improperly to affect or influence any act or decision.

C. Payment

The FCPA prohibits paying, offering, promising to pay (or authorizing to pay or offer) money or anything of value.

D. Recipient

The prohibition extends only to corrupt payments to a *foreign official, a foreign political party or party official,* or any candidate for foreign political office. A "foreign official" means any officer or employee of a foreign government, a public international organization, or any department or agency thereof, or any person acting in an official capacity. You should consider utilizing the Department of Justice's Foreign Corrupt Practices Act Opinion Procedure for particular questions as to the definition of a "foreign official," such as whether a member of a royal family, a member of a legislative body, or an official of a state-owned business enterprise would be considered a "foreign official."

The FCPA applies to payments to *any* public official, regardless of rank or position. The FCPA focuses on the *purpose* of the payment instead of the particular duties of the official receiving the payment, offer, or promise of payment, and there are exceptions to the antibribery provision for "facilitating payments for routine governmental action" (see below).

E. Business Purpose Test

The FCPA prohibits payments made in order to assist the firm in *obtaining* or *retaining business* for or with, or *directing business* to, any person. The Department of Justice interprets "obtaining or retaining business" broadly, such that the term encompasses more than the mere award or renewal of a contract. It should be noted that the business to be obtained or retained does *not* need to be with a foreign government or foreign government instrumentality.

Third Party Payments

The FCPA prohibits corrupt payments through intermediaries. It is unlawful to make a payment to a third party, while knowing that all or a portion of the payment will go directly or indirectly to a foreign official. *The term "knowing" includes conscious disregard and deliberate ignorance.* The elements of an offense are essentially the same as described above, except that in this case the "recipient" is the intermediary who is making the payment to the requisite "foreign official."

Intermediaries may include joint venture partners or agents. To avoid being held liable for corrupt third party payments, U.S. companies are encouraged to exercise due diligence and to take all necessary precautions to ensure that they have formed a business relationship with reputable and qualified partners and representatives. Such due diligence may include investigating potential foreign representatives and joint venture partners to determine if they are in fact qualified for the position, whether they have personal or professional ties to the government, the number and reputation of their clientele, and their reputation with the U.S. Embassy or Consulate and with local bankers, clients, and other business associates. In addition, in negotiating a business relationship, the U.S. firm should be aware of so-called "red flags," *i.e.*, unusual payment patterns or financial arrangements, a history of corruption in the country, a refusal by the foreign joint venture partner or representative to provide a certification that it will not take any action in furtherance of an unlawful offer, promise, or payment to a foreign public official and not take any act that would cause the U.S. firm to be in violation of the FCPA, unusually high commissions, lack of transparency in expenses and accounting records, apparent lack of qualifications or resources on the part of the joint venture partner or representative to perform the services offered, and whether the joint venture partner or representative has been recommended by an official of the potential governmental customer.

You should seek the advice of counsel and consider utilizing the Department of Justice's Foreign Corrupt Practices Act Opinion Procedure for particular questions relating to third party payments.

Permissible Payments and Affirmative Defenses

The FCPA contains an explicit exception to the bribery prohibition for "facilitating payments" for "routine governmental action" and provides affirmative defenses which can be used to defend against alleged violations of the FCPA.

Facilitating Payments for Routine Governmental Actions

There is an exception to the antibribery prohibition for payments to facilitate or expedite performance of a "routine governmental action." The statute lists the following examples: obtaining permits, licenses, or other official documents; processing governmental papers, such as visas and work orders; providing police protection, mail pick-up and delivery; providing phone service, power and water supply, loading and unloading cargo, or protecting perishable products; and scheduling inspections associated with contract performance or transit of goods across country.

Actions "similar" to these are also covered by this exception. If you have a question about whether a payment falls within the exception, you should consult with counsel. You should also consider whether to utilize the Justice Department's Foreign Corrupt Practices Opinion Procedure [described under the heading "Guidance from the Government"].

"Routine governmental action" does *not* include any decision by a foreign official to award new business or to continue business with a particular party.

Affirmative Defenses

A person charged with a violation of the FCPA's antibribery provisions may assert as a defense that the payment was lawful under the written laws of the foreign country or that the money was spent as part of demonstrating a product or performing a contractual obligation.

Whether a payment was lawful under the written laws of the foreign country may be difficult to determine. You should consider seeking the advice of counsel or utilizing the Department of Justice's Foreign Corrupt Practices Act Opinion Procedure when faced with an issue of the legality of such a payment.

Moreover, because these defenses are "affirmative defenses," the defendant is required to show in the first instance that the payment met these requirements. The prosecution does not bear the burden of demonstrating in the first instance that the payments did not constitute this type of payment.

Sanctions against Bribery

Criminal

The following criminal penalties may be imposed for violations of the FCPA's anti-bribery provisions: corporations and other business entities are subject to a fine of up to $2,000,000; officers, directors, stockholders, employees, and agents are subject to a fine of up to $100,000 and imprisonment for up to five years. Moreover, under the Alternative Fines Act, these fines may be actually quite higher—the actual fine may be up to twice the benefit that the defendant sought to obtain by making the corrupt payment. You should also be aware that fines imposed on individuals may *not* be paid by their employer or principal.

Civil

The Attorney General or the SEC, as appropriate, may bring a civil action for a fine of up to $10,000 against any firm *as well as* any officer, director, employee, or agent of a firm, or stockholder acting on behalf of the firm, who violates the antibribery provisions. In addition, in an SEC enforcement action, the court may impose an additional fine not to exceed the greater of (i) the gross amount of the pecuniary gain to the defendant as a result of the violation, or (ii) a specified dollar limitation. The specified dollar limitations are based on the egregiousness of the violation, ranging from $5,000 to $100,000 for a natural person and $50,000 to $500,000 for any other person.

The Attorney General or the SEC, as appropriate, may also bring a civil action to enjoin any act or practice of a firm whenever it appears that the firm (or an officer, director, employee, agent, or stockholder acting on behalf of the firm) is in violation (or about to be) of the antibribery provisions.

Other Governmental Action

Under guidelines issued by the Office of Management and Budget, a person or firm found in violation of the FCPA may be barred from doing business with the Federal government. *Indictment alone can lead to suspension of the right to do business with the government.* The President has directed that no executive agency shall allow any party to participate in any procurement or nonprocurement activity if any agency has debarred, suspended, or otherwise excluded that party from participation in a procurement or nonprocurement activity.

In addition, a person or firm found guilty of violating the FCPA may be ruled ineligible to receive export licenses; the SEC may suspend or bar persons from the securities business and impose civil penalties on persons in the securities business for violations of the FCPA; the Commodity Futures Trading Commission and the Overseas Private Investment Corporation both provide for possible suspension or debarment from agency programs for violation of the FCPA; and a payment made to a foreign government official that is unlawful under the FCPA cannot be deducted under the tax laws as a business expense.

Private Cause of Action

Conduct that violates the antibribery provisions of the FCPA may also give rise to a private cause of action for treble damages under the Racketeer Influenced and Corrupt Organizations Act (RICO), or to actions under other federal or state laws. For example, an action might be brought under RICO by a competitor who alleges that the bribery caused the defendant to win a foreign contract.

Guidance from the Government

The Department of Justice has established a Foreign Corrupt Practices Act Opinion Procedure by which any U.S. company or national may request a statement of the Justice Department's present enforcement intentions under the antibribery provisions of the FCPA regarding any proposed business conduct. The details of the opinion procedure may be found at 28 CFR Part 80. Under this procedure, the Attorney General will issue an opinion in response to a specific inquiry from a person or firm within thirty days of the request. (The thirty-day period does not run until the Department of Justice has received all the information it requires to issue the opinion.) Conduct for which the Department of Justice has issued an opinion stating that the conduct conforms with current enforcement policy will be entitled to a presumption, in any subsequent enforcement action, of conformity with the FCPA. Copies of releases issued regarding previous opinions are available on the Department of Justice's FCPA web site.

For further information from the Department of Justice about the FCPA and the Foreign Corrupt Practices Act Opinion Procedure, contact Peter B. Clark, Deputy Chief, or Philip Urofsky, Senior Trial Attorney, Fraud Section, Criminal Division, U.S. Department of Justice, P.O. Box. 28188, McPherson Square, Washington, D.C. 20038, (202) 514-7023.

Although the Department of Commerce has no enforcement role with respect to the FCPA, it supplies general guidance to U.S. exporters who have questions about the FCPA and about international developments concerning the FCPA. For further information from the Department of Commerce about the FCPA contact Eleanor Roberts Lewis, Chief Counsel for International Commerce, or Arthur Aronoff, Senior Counsel, Office of the Chief Counsel for International Commerce, U.S. Department of Commerce, Room 5882, 14th Street and Constitution Avenue, N.W., Washington, D.C. 20230, (202) 482-0937.

Political Risk Overview

Political Risk Insurance Update: 2000 and Beyond

As the twentieth century comes to a close, U.S. companies are increasing their overseas trade and investment activities (The World Academy, April 2009). However, the recent wars in Bosnia, the Persian Gulf, the Caribbean, and Central America (Panama) heightened executives' concerns over the risk of political instability. During the last decade, Bosnia, Argentina/England, the Tiananmen Square incident, the Panama invasion, instability in Indonesia, the turmoil in Central and West Africa, and similar events have caused many a sleepless night for senior corporate executives.

Political risk insurance is available to ease these concerns and provide stable international activity and investments. There are a host of willing brokers and underwriters anxious to manage and deal with political risk exposures. This chapter reviews the insurance options.

History

To understand the current political risk insurance arena, it is helpful to understand some of the history of this relatively new line of insurance. The first modern political risk policies were written in the early 1960s. Over the years, political risk policies have become clearer and more specific regarding the intent and scope of coverage. In some instances, these changes broadened coverage, while they made the policies more restrictive in others. The marketplace has also undergone changes over time. Ten to fifteen years ago there were many insurers and reinsurers participating in the political risk insurance marketplace; today there are only a handful.

Perhaps the greatest change in political risk insurance since its inception is the underwriting approach used. Today, underwriters have strong skills in international trading, finance, and banking combined with underwriting expertise in international insurance. A political risk insurance underwriter must understand international trade first and underwriting second. To underwrite the vanilla-type of political risk policy, such as one covering confiscation and nationalization, a basic understanding of international trade is necessary. For more complicated risks, such as counter trade, currency inconvertibility, and contract frustration, the underwriter must be well educated in the art and science of international trade. Knowledge of banking, letters of credit, foreign contract negotiation, and international law is a prerequisite for successful underwriting. Because there are no formal schools that provide training in political risk insurance, insurers have developed their own training and education programs, and many of them are excellent.

Today's highly educated underwriters require much more information than did their counterparts ten or more years ago. They ask hard, detailed questions. They also review copies of contracts and terms of trade in order to completely understand the transaction before binding coverage.

While the political risk insurance marketplace has waxed and waned over the years, the future looks bright. The insurers are positioned for effective underwriting and creative marketing to respond to the needs of U.S. companies engaged in international trade.

Spread of Risk

As with any line of insurance, it is important for insurers to achieve a spread of risk in their insurance portfolios in order to offer stable pricing and policy terms. Unfortunately, however, the buyers of this insurance have a natural tendency toward adverse selection, i.e., corporations with sales or assets in a variety of markets or countries tend to insure only the political risks associated with those areas of the world that present current political instability. The tendency of exporters/insureds to retain "easier" risks while transferring "hot spots" to insurers frustrates insurers' attempts to maintain a diverse spread of risk.

However, there is an inherent flaw in this philosophy of insuring only the difficult risks and retaining the less risky exposures. If an underwriter is provided with a broad spread of risk, a reduction of rates and more liberal underwriting terms may be obtained. The greater the spread of risk presented to an underwriter, the lower the rate that will be used to develop premium, up to a point. This may allow the insurance of more risk for the same premium than would be charged to cover only those countries, projects, or products that present the most exposure to the exporter.

There are several ways an exporter/insured can provide insurers with a spread of risk when buying political risk insurance, including the following:

Diversification of Countries. Consider insuring all export sales, even sales to countries with a tradition of political and economic stability.

Diversification of Products. Insure all products and not just those presenting the highest risk of loss.

Terms of Sale/Payment. Some methods of sale and payment present greater exposure than others. The most secure type of sale is one that has some form of guarantee, security, or collateral from an independent third party facility, such as a letter of credit where a third-party banking facility guarantees the financial aspects of the transaction. However, a significantly higher exposure is presented to the exporter/insured when sales are done on an open account, site draft consignment, or other terms whereby the customer in the third world country is likely to receive the merchandise before being obligated to pay. By insuring secured sales along with those that have no third-party guarantee, the spread of risk is increased.

Timing. Spread of risk can be increased by making shipments over an extended period of time as opposed to adhering to a compact shipping schedule. This approach allows time for some shipments to be paid for before other shipments are delivered. Adjusting the timing in this manner avoids exposing the entire value of the transaction at one time. Shipping schedules encompassing a one-to three-year period are viewed favorably by many underwriters, but some types of transactions will benefit from a longer period (e.g., seven years).

Political Risk Coverages

There are several types of political risks:

- Confiscation
- Currency inconvertibility
- Nationalization
- Devaluation
- Expropriation
- Unfair calling of financial guarantee
- Deprivation
- Trade disruptions
- War, strikes, riots, and civil commotion
- Terrorism
- Contract frustration

There are a number of different types of political risk coverages. In many respects, political risk insurance is similar to export credit insurance (and some people might include export credit insurance in the list); however, there are some distinct differences between these two categories of insurance. Basically, a political risk loss results from a peril originating out of a political or government eventuality, whether the consignee is a sovereign or private entity. An export credit risk, on the other hand, is typically defined as the credit exposure emanating solely from the actions or inactions of the private buyer.

The main distinction is that credit exposures emanating solely from private buyers are inherently more volatile than those that depend on the action of a governmental entity. This results in fewer insurers willing to write export credit coverage. When it is provided, a substantial volume of underwriting and credit information is required, the rates are high, and the coverage terms are restrictive.

Incidents such as the Gulf War and Bosnia caused many people to focus on war and terrorism coverage. Virtually all property insurance policies contain war exclusions, making it clear that damage caused by a war between two or more countries is excluded. The application of a property insurance policy to terrorist acts may not be so clear-cut, but some form of basic coverage is provided for terrorist acts by many property insurance policies. The approach used in the war exclusion of the latest Insurance Services Office, Inc. (ISO) is that commercial property forms are commonly used even in nonbureau forms. Such policies exclude only damage from war, rebellion, revolution, civil war, or warlike action of a military force. Property policies containing exclusions of this nature would typically be deemed to cover damage caused by most terrorist acts. However, some property insurance policies also exclude damage caused by a hostile or warlike action of an agent of a foreign government. Under this language, an insurer might be justified in excluding coverage if the terrorist act were proven to be inflicted by an agent of a foreign government.

ISO War Risk Exclusion

The ISO will not pay for loss or damage caused directly or indirectly by any of the following:

War and military action
1. War, including undeclared civil war
2. Warlike action by a military force, including action hindering or defending against an actual or expected attack, by any government, sovereign, or other authority using military personnel or other agents
3. Insurrection, rebellion, revolution, usurped power, or action taken by governmental authority in hindering or defending against any of these

Coverage for the excluded property damage exposures is available in the political risk insurance marketplace in the form of a war risk, civil commotion, and terrorism policy. The need for this coverage is dictated largely by the stability of the regions in which the insured's facilities are located and the scope of the war risk exclusion in the insured's property insurance policy. Of course, war risk exclusions can vary considerably from policy to policy and must be carefully analyzed when evaluating the need for separate coverage.

Confiscation, nationalization, expropriation, and deprivation (CNE&D) are the most commonly purchased political risk coverages. They are needed by organizations with assets, such as refineries or manufacturing plants, that are permanently located in other countries. The policies respond when these assets are taken over by governmental action, as recently occurred in Libya, Iraq, and Nicaragua and, in the more distant past, Chile, Vietnam, and Iran.

Nationalization takes place when the host government simply takes over an asset. Deprivation is said to occur when the host government interferes with the foreign entity's access to or utilization of its asset without actually taking possession of it. In either situation, the property owner can suffer a substantial financial loss. Confiscation and expropriation are similar actions; the host government takes over the foreign asset with the intent of returning it to the owner in the future. However, the time frame is usually not specified and often extends over several years, causing financial loss to the foreign-based property owner. Because of the similarities between these exposures, the best approach to structuring CNE&D coverage is to insure all four perils in a single policy. This approach minimizes the problems that could otherwise result from disputes with insurers as to whether a particular action falls into one category or another.

Another common political risk for which insurance is available is contract frustration. This entails the nonperformance or frustration of a contract with a host government entity or private buyer in a third world country as a result of an invalid action. An invalid action is an activity detrimental to the U.S. interest that would be considered inappropriate or illegal in the United States. It can be further defined as an action that wrongfully invalidates an overseas transaction in such a manner that the exporter is unable to obtain payment for its product or recoup its assets.

As an example of the contract frustration exposure, assume a U.S. company has a contract with a third world government to supply custom-designed parts for the construction of a factory. However the third world government cancels the contract without a valid reason prior to delivery of the product. In such a situation, it would be common for the firm to have spent a substantial sum on the initial design and preparation to manufacture the parts. Because the project involved a custom design, it is unlikely that another buyer for the parts could be found, and the exporter would suffer a financial loss.

Currency inconvertibility is an increasing concern for U.S. exporters, particularly those that sell on open account or provide open terms of payment. This type of loss occurs when the insured's customer pays in local currency, and the local government is unable to exchange the local dollars into foreign currency. Examples of countries where this can be a problem are Colombia, Brazil, Nigeria, the Philippines, and Mexico.

Currency inconvertibility has become a particular problem in countries that underwent a tremendous expansion in the 1960s through to the year 2000 because of foreign oil sales and the growth of foreign direct investment. When oil sales began to decline in the 1980s and OPEC could not agree on pricing and sales quotas, affected countries suffered a trade imbalance, causing more hard dollars to leave the country than were arriving. This made it difficult for the national banks of these countries to convert the local currency into the currency of other countries because the banks were not able to purchase foreign dollars, yen, Swiss francs, etc., with hard currency. In other words, the banks may not possess an adequate amount of U.S. dollars or other currencies to make the exchange. Ultimately, what typically occurs in these situations is a rescheduling of the country's debt over a multiyear period, implementation of strict economic controls internally within that country, and involvement by various international entities, such as the IMF, World Bank, and General Agreements on Trade and Tariff (GATT).

When insuring a trading activity in a country that commonly has problems converting its currency, underwriters typically will write the policies with a waiting period that corresponds with the time frame over which the conversion will occur.

This waiting period ranges anywhere from 60 to 720 days. The purpose of the waiting period is to ensure the coverage applies only to fortuitous loss.

An often overlooked exposure of many companies doing business overseas is the risk of an unfair calling of a financial guarantee. This risk usually arises with large transactions that take many months or years to complete. In such a situation, it is common for the buyer to make a down payment (e.g., 15 percent of the contract price), followed by periodic installment payments as the project progresses. The buyer would typically require the seller to post a letter of credit or other financial guarantee against these payments, and the buyer would be able to draw down on that letter of credit in the event something occurred that caused the supplier to default. The unfair calling of this financial guarantee is an exposure to the exporter/supplier, and unfair calling insurance protects the exporter against this risk.

Trade Disruption

Another exposure that companies involved in international trade often overlook is the business interruption exposure caused not by physical damage to a plant or other facility, but by a political event. Both importers and exporters face this loss exposure. For example, assume a manufacturer relies on a single supplier in a third world country to provide raw material that it imports for its U.S. manufacturing plants. A political occurrence, such as a war, strike, change in government, confiscation of the supplier's assets, change in politics, or change in law occurring in the source country, could disrupt the flow of that raw material into the United States. The manufacturer's ability to produce the finished product would be impaired, and a substantial financial loss may occur if an alternative source of the raw material could not be found. In a similar fashion, an exporter can experience a loss when the product is not delivered on time because of some event beyond the control of the exporter. Such exposures are insurable in the political risk insurance market.

It is important to understand that most executives tend to view their potential loss as the value of the physical product, failing to consider the potential loss of earnings, extra expense, loss of profits, and loss of market in the event a physical and/or political eventuality occurs. Trade disruption coverage can provide protection for these losses.

Markets

The political risk insurance marketplace can be divided into two basic categories: government markets and private markets. In the United States, the principal government market is the FCIA (Foreign Credit Insurance Association, now part of the Great American Insurance Company), which was authorized through the U.S. government via Ex-Im Bank. With headquarters in New York City and satellite offices throughout the United States, the FCIA provides many types of political risk coverage as well as export credit insurance for U.S. exporters shipping U.S. products to approved countries. Most non-Communist countries in the world that have favorable trading status with the United States are considered approved.

In the past, the FCIA was considered bureaucratic and unresponsive to the needs of most exporters. However, in recent years, this has changed, and the FCIA has become more responsive by offering competitive and comprehensive programs, such as the bank letter of credit and new-to-export buyer programs.

OPIC (Overseas Private Investment Corporation) is the other U.S. government-sponsored market for political risk insurance. OPIC insures U.S. nonmilitary investment exposures, such as confiscation and nationalization, in developing nations throughout the world. Its terms and conditions are broad, and the rates are as competitive as the FCIA's. However, only assets located in nations having favorable trade relationships with the United States qualify for coverage with OPIC.

There are two drawbacks to the U.S. government programs. First, they are subject to U.S. diplomatic and trade policies. When the U.S. government is following a restrictive trade policy with a particular country, the Ex-Im Bank and other government facilities tend to follow suit, thus reducing the availability of coverage or restricting coverage terms for that country. Likewise, when the government eases trade restrictions with a country, coverage availability and terms will increase.

While this may be good politics, it sometimes restricts coverage availability for transactions with countries that, while not on favorable trade terms with the United States, might present good business opportunities and be excellent credit risks for individual businesses. For example, a number of U.S. companies have been very successful in trading with the Soviet Union over the last few years and have been paid regularly and responsibly. Because, however, of its unfavorable trade relationship with the United States, transactions with the Soviet Union are generally not eligible for most of the U.S. government's insurance programs.

The second drawback to U.S. government markets is that they only cover U.S. companies and/or products. As an example of how this restricts availability, consider a firm located in New York City staffed by U.S. personnel that exports Canadian products into Europe on an open account basis, thus creating an exposure that could be covered by export credit insurance. This company would not be eligible to buy credit insurance from the U.S. government facilities because the product is not manufactured in the United States.

Of course, this limitation of coverage availability is fundamental to the underlying purpose for which Ex-Im Bank and OPIC was created: To encourage and support the exportation of U.S. products and services. These facilities are not always profitable, but provide an indirect means of subsidizing U.S. business interests overseas. At this time, the U.S. government will only subsidize activity that directly benefits U.S. interests, products, or services.

Most other Western nations also have established facilities similar to the Ex-Im Bank and OPIC to insure export sales to other countries. U.S. companies with divisions domiciled in these nations can often access these local government programs.

The private insurance market provides coverages that are not available from the government markets, and it is not bound by the diplomatic policy of any one nation. This market is basically made up of some U.S.-domiciled insurance companies and London markets. The principal U.S. companies that write political risk insurance are Chubb, CNA, and American International Underwriters (AIU), but there are a handful of other insurers that occasionally write various types of political risk coverage. Most U.S. insurance companies with marine capability will write war, strikes, riots, and civil commotion coverages on overseas transactions. Along with Chubb and AIU, other underwriters include MOAC (Continental), CIGNA, Fireman's Fund, and Great American.

Being commercially driven, U.S. insurers will write insurance in those areas where there is an opportunity for profit. The natural downside of this tendency is that it is difficult to obtain insurance from these insurers in countries where the possibility of loss is significant. In general, however, U.S. insurers offer broad policies and competitive rates and are willing to write on a spread-of-risk basis, affording the exporter a complete program covering all overseas sales.

The London market is composed of Lloyd's of London, Institute of London Underwriters (ILU), and other insurers. This marketplace is as competitive as its U.S. counterpart. In addition, the London insurers typically are willing to put out more capacity and are more agreeable to manuscripting policy forms. London underwriters also have different perspectives on certain areas of the world than their U.S. counterparts and may provide coverage in areas where U.S. insurers are reluctant to do so.

Care should be taken in choosing an agent or broker to access the marketplace. The broker should be large enough to bring a substantial number of international resources to the table and have a staff that is knowledgeable in international trade and the political risk marketplace.

Loss Control

There are a number of loss control tactics that U.S. companies doing business overseas should consider using. These measures will help reduce exposure and secure more competitive pricing and more comprehensive terms from political risk insurers.

Political risk exposures are heavily influenced by the contracts underlying the business transaction. All too often, contracts are executed on overseas transactions without review by insurance advisers. Knowledgeable insurance advisers often can suggest alterations that will substantially reduce the exposure, making the transaction easier and less costly to insure. For example, underwriters view the inclusion of arbitration clauses favorably because such clauses substantially increase the likelihood that the exporter will get a fair hearing in the event of a dispute, as opposed to arguing its case in the local courts. Consider a situation in which an exporter is fighting the government of a third world country on an unfair calling of a financial guarantee in that country's court. There would be a serious disadvantage to the U.S. firm in that situation compared to an arbitration proceeding in Zurich, London, or some other city outside that government.

Another consideration is to give the local government an interest in the overseas venture. For example, assume a U.S. firm builds a plant in a third world country.

Involving local personnel in the management and operations of a local venture can also reduce the political risk exposures. When a foreign-owned facility employs many local citizens, the government is less inclined to cause a disruption of its operations.

Careful consideration should be given to the currency transactions specified by the contract. A transaction that runs into problems because it requires that local currency be converted into U.S. dollars might flow more smoothly if some other currency, such as yen or marks, could be used to complete the deal. The alternative currency might then be used in other international trades or converted to U.S. dollars.

It is also important to set up contingency plans to follow in the event a political eventuality occurs that would disrupt the venture or transaction. This involves developing specific strategies for dealing with potential political problems.

Global Risk Management

Political Risk Coverage Analyzed: Ten Critical Steps for Risk Managers

With more corporations making direct investments overseas, increasing foreign sales activities, and dealing more frequently with third world countries, the political risk exposure has increased, creating a need for risk managers to direct attention to this subject area (Thomas A. Cook, White Paper).

Political risk exposures generally refer to losses emanating from government or political sources. They include confiscation, nationalization, expropriation, and depravation of assets by foreign governments; import/export license cancellations; currency inconvertibility; war; strikes, riot, and civil commotions; embargo; contract cancellation/repudiation; and boycott. Losses emanating from business dealing with private entities abroad are generally classified as export/credit exposures. Insurance can be purchased against one or all of these risks. Following are ten critical steps that a risk manager should take when purchasing political risk insurance:

1. **Selecting a Broker/Underwriter.** The choice of a broker is perhaps the risk manager's most important concern, because the broker is the first line of contact. There are many brokers who can talk around the subject of political risks, but there are few who can perform adequately in a limited insurance market.

   There are few options in the choice of underwriting market today, but the number is increasing rapidly as more insurance companies enter the political risk arena to meet the demands of American businesses.

   A properly selected broker/underwriter combination will maximize risk management effectiveness. Establishing broker/underwriter rapport will help accomplish mutual understanding, reliable service, continuity of coverage, and increased opportunities for competitive pricing.

2. **Service Requirements.** In the process of selecting a broker and underwriter, an analysis must be made of what the corporate entity is looking for in the relationship. Aside from arranging the protection of assets, other services available include:
   - Export financing
   - Filing of applications
   - Political risk intelligence
   - Loss control and claims handling
   - Contract and exposure review
   - Communication of coverage to divisions, subsidiaries, etc.

   The servicing area for political risk varies greatly among brokers, underwriters, and specialty consultants. Commissions and fees that affect the bottom line should reflect the services provided and the ultimate decision in a choice of broker and market.

3. **Combining Risks.** Risk managers should combine various political risk exposures under one policy. This will maximize underwriting clout in obtaining favorable terms and conditions and will greatly help to reduce premiums. Underwriters will favor a spread of risk and react positively toward being the corporation's only political risk market.

   Because of the limited number of markets, minimal capacity, and a small underwriting/brokerage political risk community, it makes good risk management sense to concentrate risks into one market and not continually seek competition.

   Risk managers also should combine other international risks in the coverage such as kidnap and ransom, difference in conditions, business interruption, marine, construction all-risk, etc. Underwriters favorably view combining these insurances in a package policy, because they typically are more stable and predictable than other political risks and help provide more reasons for the market to perform.

4. Communication. Because political risk insurances are unique and cannot be explained to the layman as easily as other conventional property/liability coverages, there is an absolute need to establish comprehensive communication channels between the risk manager's office and operating units such as international sales, treasury, corporate finance and credit, and legal, to name a few. The following actions are recommended:
  – Set up in-house seminars to educate and inform employees.
  – Establish formal communication systems, including updates and weekly status reports.
  – Appoint local coordinators to become familiar with the subject area and operating plan if, because of distant operating units, logistics present problems.
  – Consider having brokers communicate directly with the divisional/operating personnel. This might expedite information transfers and provide additional support. However, the risk manager should always be kept informed of activity.

5. Contract Review. The typical method of providing underwriting data to the market is through questionnaires. This is an excellent starting point; however, a thorough review should always include analysis and review of the contract, terms of sale, terms of payment, and other documents relating to the exposure. This will help assure that the proper coverage is obtained, the underwriter thoroughly understands the risks, and any questions as to intent are answered clearly.

   Changes often can be obtained by altering contract wording, terms of sale, etc., which could greatly reduce exposure and/or increase underwriting ability.

6. Political Risk Intelligence. Political risk insurance focuses on economic, social, and political events. To assess the need for coverage, the exposures must be understood, and understanding the exposures requires information. There are numerous sources of international intelligence, including the U.S. State and Commerce Departments, private information services, banks, trade associations, embassies, and the media. As part of brokerage services, qualified facilities will assist in the area of information support and provide up-to-date intelligence on world conditions.

7. Rates, Terms, Conditions. Consider that each market's standard policy is different and that manuscripting is a necessity if proper coverage is to be provided. The exact exposure should be explicitly defined, and coverage should be tailored to meet the risk, whether it be for nationalization, currency inconvertibility, license cancellation, war, etc. Other areas that should be addressed are:
  – Deductibles and coinsurance
  – Waiting period
  – Rescheduling
  – Warranties and exclusions

- Method of reporting of exposures
- Coverage for business interruption and protection of profits
- Loss of market, delay
- Changes or fluctuations in currency, which is an area for which it is becoming more difficult, if not impossible, to arrange coverage
- Currency for claims payments
- War risks
- Cost that appears to be controlled by market conditions, current economic and political situations, and quality of presentation is typically a significant corporate expenditure.
- Premiums vary greatly with each risk, but one must be assured that apples are not being compared with oranges. Compiling checklists comparing quotas is a good method for fair evaluation.

8. **Export Credit.** Most political risk coverages exclude export credit (the proximate cause of loss emanates from the private buyer). Risks such as nonpayment and contract frustration are significant exposures that exist when dealing with private buyers. It is important to determine whether the ultimate buyer is private or governmental, as interests may be jointly held. The time to make this determination is before the policy is secured and not after a loss has occurred.

   Markets for export credit coverage are more limited than for political risk, requiring specific underwriting details about the creditworthiness of the buyer and the payment track record. Obtaining this insurance is often a tool for increasing foreign sales, because account receivables are protected and banks are more apt to provide lucrative export financing.

9. **Loss Control.** Insureds should seek measures to minimize opportunity for loss and to entice the interest of local businesses. Such measures include:
   - Utilization of local management, personnel, etc.
   - Development of sales that require continuing support, like providing service, maintenance, spare parts, accessories, etc.
   - Development of rapport with local officials by joining business associations, trade groups, etc.
   - Review of opportunities for local financing of the import or project
   - Analysis of the contract to further protect interests or secure favorable treatment from the host country

   All of these will help control the fate of your venture in the event of a loss.

10. **Claims Procedures.** Before a loss, written procedures should be developed addressing the who, what, when, where, and how of handling claims. List all personnel of the broker and the underwriter and include their home phone numbers. Contingency plans should be developed to provide options in the event of loss so that business will stay on track with little interruption. Run

drills and have meetings with key personnel. Procedures should be agreed to ahead of time to arrange for arbitrators in the event of contractual and/or claims disputes.

Use a Specialist to Arrange International Protection

The Export Trading Act of 1982 made it easier for the small- to medium-size company to do business overseas. To be competitive, these companies have to sell on terms where credit is extended beyond transfer of title or alternative credit/financing terms are offered. This poses two significant exposures: contingent marine and political/export credit. The inexperienced exporter typically overlooks these exposures until there is a loss. Additionally, U.S. exporters are selling on terms where the importer is controlling insurance, i.e., cost and freight (C&F), free on board (FOB), free alongside (FAS), etc., and has terms of payment extended beyond the ocean voyage or after arrival at the ultimate destination.

The marine insurance problem arises when a loss occurs that is discovered at the final destination, and the buyer refuses payment or partial payment based on the fact that not all the merchandise has arrived or is not in 100 percent sound condition.

The exporter will advise the buyer that the full quantity of a sound product was shipped, and that the buyer should seek payment from its insurance company. However, the buyer may never have arranged insurance or may have limited terms and conditions not covering this type of loss, or the policy may have a huge deductible. Whatever the reason, the buyer has the merchandise and has not paid for it. Other than litigation, there are few other means to seek indemnification from the loss. This is where the marine insurance policy can play a strategic role.

There are numerous insurance brokerage companies that specialize in managing these exposures.

An exporter who sells on terms where it does not control insurance and can sustain a financial loss as a result of physical loss or damage can arrange a "contingency cover" that will respond to the loss as if the exporter was insuring the cargo as a primary interest. This insurance is known as "unpaid vendor" cover and can be easily arranged as part of the master cargo policy or on an independent special risk basis. This area is where most exporters leave the door open for exposure and most brokers and underwriters miss the boat. It takes a unique and specialized understanding of marine cargo logistics to do it well.

Specialized insurance brokers highlight other exposures such as political risk/export credit that may even be more significant, as it is a primary and direct source of loss, not "contingent."

The risks faced come under a multitude of titles: import export license cancellation, private buyer guarantees, currency inconvertibility, confiscation, expropriation, war risk debt rescheduling, contract frustration, letter of credit drawdown, consequential damages, nationalization, deprivation, strikes, riots, and civil commotion.

Increasing those exposures is the U.S. exporter's need to deal with the third world political events in Iran. Afghanistan, Lebanon, Mexico, Nigeria, and Brazil have increased the demand for facilities to allow exporting corporations to transfer their risks.

There are numerous government and private insurance companies available to underwrite the political and export credit exposures. Lloyds of London underwrites a multitude of U.S. exporter exposures.

An increasing number of U.S. companies are participating in foreign government purchases and investments. The contracts involved have inherent political risk exposures. What if a foreign government, after placing a $3-million order and after 10 months of production (generating expenses of $1.5 million), experiences a coup d'état? The new government cancels the contract. Because of the nature of the sale, only $250,000 of the $1.5 million already expended can be salvaged, bringing the net loss to $1.25 million. This risk could have been insured.

What about the U.S. exporter who sells on consignment to Central America and ninety days after arrival the private buyer has not paid or the customer has paid, but because of a trade deficit, the state bank is unable to convert currency? Where does that exporter turn for collection? These risks are insurable.

Political and export credit insurance can be expensive, and developing underwriting data is time-consuming; however, the exposure warrants the effort and expense because of the protection it provides from potential disaster.

Policies typically have deductible and coinsurance levels with long waiting periods between time of default and underwriters claim payment. These terms should be negotiated in accordance with your contractual obligations.

Terms and conditions vary from underwriter to underwriter, and competent brokerage support is mandatory to negotiate the most comprehensive coverage for a particular client's needs. There are only a handful of competent insurance brokers. When choosing a broker, the exporter should review the broker's capability to place the coverage and also provide a country risk analysis, analyze sales contracts, work with international marketing executives, service the account daily, and assist in claims settlement.

Many U.S. exporters have used their policies in conjunction with export financing facilities to arrange lucrative export financing and have found this transfer of risk to be an avenue to increased foreign sales.

An exporting executive has the responsibility to protect the corporation's assets. The application of contingent marine insurance and political risk/export credit covers are prudent steps in the overall functions of exporting management. The bottom line is protection of assets and profit and the opportunity to become more competitive in international sales.

Information and Technology in Sales Management
*World Trade Institute**

With the rapid growth of sales automation and such online technologies as Lotus Notes and intranets, many corporations have rushed to deploy systems for distributing information and documents of all kinds to their salespeople. As markets and products change with accelerating pace, salespeople must assimilate and apply vast amounts of current information about their markets, their competition, and the solutions they can offer to customers. The recognition that salespeople are knowledge workers, perhaps the most overburdened of all, is gradually dawning on senior sales and marketing executives in the most forward-thinking companies. It is becoming obvious to such executives that knowledgeable salespeople can offer a significant competitive advantage at every stage of the sales process. Knowledge of customers' business issues, market dynamics, company vision, the competition, sales strategy, and products or services themselves helps salespeople establish and maintain credibility. They can identify the customer's pressing needs and configure optimal solutions, sell the benefits of those solutions, and guard against competitive challenges.

On the other hand, those working today in nearly all functions within business organizations suffer from severe information overload. Salespeople are perhaps the most overloaded of all. Information of many types, in many different forms and media, pours in on the salesperson. Dozens or even hundreds of documents are intended to provide salespeople with the knowledge they need to compete. Yet because the information generally arrives from many different sources, neither its content nor format is consistent. Sales guides, training materials, audio and video tapes, sets of overhead transparencies, sales collateral, proposals, memos, emails, and now documents in online databases often cover the same ground in slightly different ways, and are often very difficult to use if one is in a hurry to find needed information. The result is a scarcity of knowledge in an abundance of information.

By default, most salespeople pick up the phone or seek the most convenient source of answers to their questions, e.g., the product manager's latest slide set or a brochure intended for customers. Salespeople in some companies may make as many as 20–30 phone calls before they get the knowledge they need in response to specific questions. Product managers and their staff may respond to literally hundreds of phone calls and emails per week with answers to questions that they have already answered in some form or other, spending as much as 70% of their time doing so. These same marketing professionals also devote substantial portions of their work weeks to creating all kinds of "sales knowledge deliverables," whether in the form of training materials, white papers, product briefs, competitive updates, or sales guides. We often find literally dozens of documents covering similar topics written

---

* (Reprinted with permission from The World Trade Institute, New York City, June 2000.)

by multiple people within organizations. Lists of key messages and benefits differ for the same product, and the management and updating of information become nearly impossible. Thus, rather than maintaining a single, coherent knowledge base, the sources tend to create yet more documents in a near-futile effort to update the field.

The overall result is that companies invest huge amounts in product development, marketing, and sales support, yet the messages that get to the sales force are so inconsistent that the return on those investments is not what it could be.

Needed: Fluent Access to and Use of Sales Knowledge

To the extent that salespeople must compete based on the added value of their knowledge, they must be able to easily access, learn, and apply knowledge. They may or may not need large amounts of knowledge, depending on their products, markets, and sales/marketing strategies. But certainly they need the right knowledge—those facts, questions, answers, descriptions, and other knowledge nuggets that will enable them to perform each key aspect of their jobs most effectively. In fact, it is the actionable nature of this knowledge—its relevance to and ability to be used in on-the-job performance—that separates it from mere information or data. Ideally, salespeople should be able to access the knowledge they need, already transformed into structures and formats relevant to sales activities while easy to apply because of its relevance and form. The days in which corporations can expect their salespeople to successfully fend for themselves in the jungle of information overload are coming to an end. Those companies that ensure easy access to sales-relevant knowledge will enable their salespeople to perform significantly better than their competitors who do not have such easy-to-access knowledge.

The Challenge of Sales Knowledge Management

Managing the knowledge of a sales and marketing organization cuts across disciplines and departments and may include various functions within Marketing, Sales, Training, Sales Automation, and Customer Service. Conscious efforts in some major corporations to build a "learning organization" have yielded such job titles as Chief Knowledge Officer (CKO) and have involved cross-functional teams of various kinds. Recognition of the problem is itself a major advance. In many companies, Sales, Marketing, and other functions do not cooperate effectively, and frequently blame one another for lack of effective communication.

The challenge is to make vast amounts of dynamic information both useful and accessible to salespeople for use in performing specific tasks on the job. This can take the form of various learning tools and programs as well as reference resources, both hard copy and online. To realize a return on their corporate knowledge assets, executives need to provide for processes and systems that will optimize the capture and use of knowledge. Because knowledge is actionable information, used to support performance, an effective solution demands cross-functional processes for collaboration and communication.

Knowledge-Management Functions

Managing knowledge in an organization requires three distinct but overlapping functions, plus processes and tools for maintaining and refreshing the knowledge base over time.

- **Access**: Salespeople must be able to access required knowledge easily, quickly, and with the confidence that they can find what they want. The classic assertion that "salespeople don't read," while it may be true as compared with university professors, is actually the consequence of most organizations' failure to provide reliable, quick access to needed knowledge. We have seen repeatedly that salespeople will literally ask for more information if given hard copy or online reference resources that support rapid, reliable access. There is something like the traditional 80/20 rule with respect to the amount of knowledge a salesperson must be able to access versus the amount he or she must actually learn. For many tasks, such as planning account strategy, preparing for sales calls, writing proposals, and organizing information for presentations, salespeople can perform well if they simply can find the needed information. They need not commit it all to memory if there is a system that allows them to rapidly find needed information.
- **Learning**: Salespeople need to learn a relatively small amount of knowledge: that which is needed face-to-face with customers or for routinely thinking through problems (e.g., key associations between potential customers' problems and product solutions). And where salespeople do need to learn, they must be able to achieve what we call fluency—that level of "second nature" knowledge that comes from regular practice.
- **Application**: To be useful, whether accessed or learned, sales knowledge must be organized and presented in a form that supports application in practical tasks. Ideally, information for salespeople will appear in formats and structures directly applicable to their jobs, e.g., issue–implications descriptions of market drivers or needs–solutions tables. Such forms of knowledge support performance without the need for salespeople to reorganize, rewrite, or otherwise reprocess available information.

Technology Solutions

Technology is often seen as a panacea for the problems of knowledge management. Computer-based training programs are among the most prominent forms of knowledge technology. Many different software technologies attempt to address the issue of knowledge access, including traditional database programs, online documentation systems, hypertext and multimedia authoring tools, expert systems, and more recently Lotus Notes groupware and HTML and Java-based Internet and intranet technologies. So-called electronic performance support systems (EPSS) combine various types of software technology in an effort to support key on-the-job tasks. Delivery mechanisms include conventional storage in desktop or portable computers, access to networks via internal LANs, intranets, or the Internet, and distribution via CD-ROM. An important requirement for field-based sales professionals is convenient and time-efficient remote access, often via telephone lines.

What is common to all of these technologies is the old adage "garbage in, garbage out." We have seen case after case where companies have naively "dumped" hundreds of documents and bits of information into one or another form of database on the premise that merely putting this information online in electronic form will enable salespeople to access. We find that such repositories are often no better than distributing information via hundreds of documents. When the information is not consistently labeled, organized, or formatted, it produces at least as much information overload as hundreds of paper documents. In fact, technology merely allows many companies to create information overload at a more rapid pace than with conventional means. In both computerized learning or access systems, the failure to identify what knowledge is actually needed for performance, to eliminate unneeded information, and to conduct analyses of how salespeople will use the knowledge neutralizes the potential benefits of technology.

Thus, technology is not a simple cure. Unless the information made available by technology is analyzed, organized, and presented in a form that optimally supports performance, it will add to rather than alleviate the problems of sales information overload. Leading-edge companies, including the suppliers of database and groupware technologies who use their own systems, are only recently coming to the stark realization that technology per se is not the solution.

Knowledge Architecture: Organizing Knowledge for Use

What is missing in nearly every effort we have seen to manage knowledge for the sales force is what we have come to call knowledge architecture: that is, a scheme for consistently and comprehensively labeling, sequencing, and structuring all the types of knowledge needed for sales. One of our clients put it most simply when she asked, "What if your newspaper were formatted and organized differently every day?" The answer, of course, is that you would find it very difficult to use and enjoy the newspaper if you could not predict how or where stock quotes, classified ads, sport statistics, entertainment news, or other important features would appear in the document. This, however, is directly analogous to how most organizations provide knowledge for their salespeople, and this is the problem our proprietary Product Knowledge Architecture™ was designed to address.

The key features of any knowledge architecture, according to our definition, include standards for:

- **Chunking and labeling**: Just as the newspaper contains predictable "chunks" of information, labeled with the same words and phrases each day, an architecture for corporate knowledge bases should contain standard definitions of the types of content needed by users and standard words or phrases for labeling them. This feature of a knowledge architecture enables users to search for, learn about, remember, and apply knowledge of various types using known language. A standard chunking and labeling scheme also allows the organization to more easily update and maintain its knowledge resources by providing a framework for determining what knowledge has changed over time.

- **Sequencing**: Standard sequences of topics, whether in reference documents, overhead transparency sets, or learning materials and presentations, support both access, or navigation, and efficient learning. The ideal is that the sequence of topics in a knowledge architecture will provide a path for first-time sequential learning, but also will allow later random access to paper or online resources.

- **Formatting**: Standard page layouts and document structures, if designed to optimally support performance, make it easy to access and learn knowledge. Structures such as standard types of tables and similarly structured diagrams, if used throughout a knowledge base, enable users to obtain knowledge in a useful form. For example, standard needs–solutions tables are far easier to access and apply than are dense text about the same topics. A mature knowledge architecture contains a range of standard formats for key types of knowledge, wherever it might occur in the organization.

- **Linking**: Standard links or cross-references connect chunks of knowledge that users may need to access or learn together, e.g., industry segments and potential customer needs. The best knowledge architectures contain standard links between related topics, a feature that is especially powerful when implemented in online technology.

It is important to recognize that, if implemented across the organization, a knowledge architecture can rationalize and improve the usefulness of a wide range of knowledge resources, including reference books and documentation, online resources, training materials and programs, marketing white papers, emails, and even audio and video tapes. Such an architecture provides the structure for systems, processes, and specific deliverables related to a particular area of knowledge and performance (e.g., sales) across the entire organization. As you will see, each of these key architectural features can be implemented in various ways with different types of software technologies.

State of the Sales Knowledge Technology Marketplace

Technologies of all kinds are available for providing sales knowledge. While there are many different forms of computerized learning/training tools, this white paper will focus more on technologies for access and application.

Sales force automation is an exploding market, with all kinds of tools available for managing the sales process in both simple and more complex situations and organizational structures. Within the scope of sales automation, the systems for providing sales knowledge are generally called either sales libraries or marketing encyclopedias.

- **Sales libraries**: This term is often used to refer to databases of one kind or another that contain all kinds of different documents and information chunks intended to support sales. Ideally, it distinguishes between sales collateral, intended primarily for customers, and sales knowledge resources, intended to inform salespeople.
- **Marketing encyclopedias**: Marketing encyclopedias, strictly speaking, should contain those materials and documents intended for customers, including brochures, proposals and letters, presentation sets, demonstrations, and other customer-focused information. In fact, most organizations that we have seen mix customer materials with resources intended for the salespeople, often without specifying which is which.

As these types of applications have begun to appear in the last several years, they have been implemented in a variety of ways, including proprietary systems designed and developed as modules in larger sales automation programs, conventional database technologies (i.e., Oracle's), Lotus Notes, and Web-based technologies using hypertext markup language (HTML) and Java in publicly accessible sites on the Worldwide Web or private intranets. In addition, a number of knowledge-classification schemes have been applied with technology designed to filter commercially available news-feed services for articles and other snippets related to key markets, customers, etc. (e.g., grapeVINE Technologies).

What is most obvious in any review of the existing sales knowledge technologies is that most of them currently comprise dumping grounds—single electronic "places" where marketing and salespeople can publish or deposit all kinds of information, much like the traditional three-ring binders containing multiple documents that sales organizations often distribute to their people. Materials and information are most often organized by document type, product name, or alphabetically. And the documents themselves are generally enormously redundant, and inconsistent in organization and content. For example, at one of our high-technology clients, we were able to find in their intranet over 160 documents related to a particular product set, representing a degree of information overload that was nearly impenetrable by salespeople in that organization. Understandably, those who create such online resources often complain of salespeople who do not use them. In fact, technology can worsen rather than improve the problem of information overload.

A final note about current technology options is that many technologists have naively believed that the problems of analyzing, organizing, and providing access (e.g., via key words) to online resources can be handled automatically using intelligent software. Various systems for parsing, keywording, and creating links automatically have been applied. However, those at the forefront of practical knowledge management for the sales force recognize that it takes human intervention and screening to meaningfully assign keywords, structure and summarize information, and create useful links. In fact, a new job classification—knowledge manager—is emerging as a critical step in the process of providing and maintaining useful knowledge and ensuring application of standards for optimal accessibility. We want salespeople to be able to select, rather than search for, needed information, and this requires that someone else has already filtered, formatted, and tagged or labeled it. Leveraging the work of a few knowledge managers for the benefit of many more salespeople can be an extremely cost-effective strategy.

Our technology strategy can be described as containing the following key elements:

Open architecture: The Product Knowledge Architecture™ is our comprehensive knowledge architecture for sales and marketing, based on nearly ten years of research and development with clients across industries. Containing seven major segments and multiple sub-segments sequenced to support both learning and access, the architecture provides standards that are customizable for each client organization for chunking and labeling sales knowledge, formatting on paper or online, and linking key sub-segments to one another. This architecture can be readily translated into the features of software systems, including keywords, views, document or database templates, and links. The Product Knowledge Architecture provides a unique and powerful framework for analyzing, organizing, and presenting information for sales in any form.

Implementation in industry standard technologies: Although the Product Knowledge Architecture can be implemented in virtually any type of online technology, we have focused on the emerging technology standards, for example Web technology and Lotus Notes. Virtually every major corporation is now using one or both of these technologies in some form, and with the recent seamless integration by Lotus/IBM of Notes with Internet technologies in Domino, these technologies provide excellent vehicles for knowledge management. Notes, in particular, with its workflow, collaboration, and document management capabilities, provides an ideal technology environment for managing sales knowledge. Beyond these industry standards, we will selectively respond to other opportunities for implementing our methodologies using other types of software.

Online FluencyBuilding™: As part of our technology strategy, we offer a Windows-based tool, ThinkFast™, for providing fun, effective FluencyBuilding practice online for fact-level knowledge. We then build upon this knowledge with noncomputerized practice such as responding to tough questions and objections, talking with overhead slides, etc.

Client partners: In the process of evolving our technology offerings, we seek client partners whose real business problems define the requirements for our systems. We have always conducted our research and development in the context of client relationships, so that our products and services represent real solutions to sales and marketing performance problems, rather than "inventing" products in a vacuum. As new technologies offer further opportunities, client situations provide the environment for achieving significant mutual benefit.

Updating and maintenance tools: Part of our strategy relates to updating and maintaining sales knowledge bases, one of the most challenging aspects of sales and marketing support. The Product Knowledge Architecture provides a framework for analysis and identification of knowledge chunks in need of updating, as well as a classification scheme for input from the field and from multiple sources within organizations. Combined with workflow technologies, we plan to develop increasingly sophisticated processes and models for maintaining the integrity and economy of virtual sales knowledge bases in our client organizations. Moreover, we will offer to serve as an outsource vendor for the maintenance function where our clients would prefer not to manage this specialized process themselves.

Process design and management: We take a systems approach to everything we do. We configure sets of products, services, and specific deliverables to meet the specific knowledge needs of our clients' salespeople in a systematic fashion. We also recognize that our client organizations will need to define new processes and job functions in order to optimize the use of technology-based solutions for sales knowledge problems. This need for process is a corollary of the "garbage in, garbage out" adage, and takes principles of process improvement and quality management into account, as they apply to knowledge systems and processes.

Integration: Whenever possible, we work with client organizations to integrate their use of technology-based solutions with other low-tech aspects of their sales knowledge efforts. For example, we encourage training departments to integrate sales training events and programs with use of online resources to encourage and support use of those resources on the job. Ideally, our client organizations come to see all efforts to provide knowledge to the field as parts of an integrated, enterprise-wide sales knowledge system.

Benefits of the Strategy

The strategy outlined in this document offers a number of benefits to any organization choosing to work with us:

- Greater integration and effectiveness of company messages to the marketplace through the sales force
- More cost-efficient development and maintenance of sales knowledge resources
- Improved information auditing, less redundancy, greater assurance of completeness in the knowledge base
- Fewer errors and inconsistencies in the knowledge base
- Less cognitive overhead for salespeople because of the consistent knowledge architecture

and the most important:

- Greater overall sales and marketing productivity

Making Someone Sell

Thomas A. Cook

ARI

First of all, we can never make someone sell. But we can lead them to sell, and we can manage their efforts.

Are good salespeople made or are they born? The reality is that it is both. With over 25 years of sales management under my belt, I believe there are many innate qualities that better salespeople are born with, such as an outgoing personality, persistence, emotional intelligence, high achiever, etc. But those inherited qualities can only take them so far. They need other skills, for which training, time, and experience can mold into sales greatness.

Yes, there are great used-car salesmen, but that is probably all they can sell. Try and sell life insurance, plastic moldings, industrial-grade air conditioners, domestic trucking services, and the like; it is another world from selling used cars. Not to say that used-car salespeople do not have some good qualities, because they do, but most of what they do and how they do it would not work in business or commerce as we know it in today's diversified economy.

The salesperson of the new millennium has to develop significant skill sets that require intelligence, creativity, and perseverance.

Good sales management is leading the salesperson to develop these skills and put them into dual value—to make money for the company and put commissions and earnings in their pockets. The sales manager accomplishes this leadership responsibility by developing realistic goals both at a corporate level and then on the individual level for each salesperson. The sales manager then develops specific strategies to accomplish those goals. The strategies are tailored to meet the capabilities and talents of the individual salesperson.

Then comes the real hard part—making sure the management structure is in place to have total accountability in a realistic time frame. Accountability measures execution and consistency, as it is those two areas that will, at the end of the day, ensure success.

Compare this to losing weight. The goal is to lose 20 pounds. The strategy is to get into a gym every day and work out for an hour. Eat sensibly and cut out all the carbs. The difficult part is executing and doing it consistently. Like in January, when all the gyms are filled with "wannabes"; by February 1 they are all gone. The goal was good. The strategy was excellent. It all failed because the execution and the consistency only lasted for a month.

Sales management is 24/7/365. Good sales management is not making them sell, but providing the leadership and the management structure to:

■ Develop sales goals
■ Develop sales strategies
■ Develop accountability systems to ensure execution
■ Develop initiatives that achieve consistent results

Sales Management Seminar: Newly Appointed Sales Manager Workshop Agenda

Thomas A. Cook

Presentation for First-Time Sales Managers

The purpose of this section in the Appendix is to provide an outline workshop presentation for newly appointed first-time managers in sales to have as a guideline on all the issues and potential resolutions.

It asks questions and allows a place for response and consideration. It also provides bullet point concepts to think about and act on. The workshop aligns itself with all the chapters in this book and the vast array of suggestions, considerations, and actions for sales managers who have newly inherited responsibilities to follow.

Why Are You in the Position of a Newly Appointed Sales Manager?

List some reasons:

■ Success at sales

- Potential or already demonstrated success in management
- Best option within or from outside interviews
- Demonstration of capabilities in other areas of the organization
- An even better salesperson who convinced senior management
- Belief and confidence in you

Why Have You Accepted the Position?

- Money
- Security
- Career opportunity

What Are Your Concerns or Fears about These New Responsibilities?

- Failure
- Coworkers: what they will think?
- Hours and time commitment
- Leadership skills
- Ability to meet goals and execute strategies

What Does Senior Management Expect from You?

- Lead the charge
- Sales
- Profits: business and costing models
- Problem solver
- New business development
- Marketing (maybe)
- Social director
- Ambassador of the organization

What Are Your Expectations from This Seminar and Class?

- Stay out of trouble
- Make you think
- Learn options and betterments
- Share methods and ways
- Assist in goals, strategies, and executions
- Make it easier for me

Management vs. Leadership?

- Difference
- Importance in understanding
- "Character" issue

Goals and Strategies

- Define each
- Corporate vs. individual
- Team vs. individual

Execution and Consistency: Success or Failure

- Importance of understanding
- Hardest park of succeeding in sales
- Commitment...Just do it

Name the Major Responsibilities of a "Sales Manager"

- Keep sales personnel on track...accountability/responsibility systems
- Interface corporte goals with sales personnel strategies
- Interface with all operations...finance, manufacturing/ops, customer service, etc.
- Troubleshoot
- Providing leads and lead sources

What Are Transitional Issues?

- Friend vs. manager
- Developing existing sales personnel
- Find new sales personnel
- Motivational issues
- Sources of motivational needs
- Developing sales skill sets: Best practices
- When to be a father, mother, sister, preacher, disciplinarian, educator, hand-holder, mentor, or friend?
- Sales and customer service
- Products vs. services

Why Do People Buy?

Management Qualities

- Good communicator
- Organized
- Understands priorities
- Time management
- Negotiation skills
- Good salesperson (maybe the best, but not necessary)
- Bridge between senior management, finance, customer service, manufacturing/ops, traffic/logistics, etc.
- Calm, stable, focused, and centered demeanor
- Consistent
- Responsible (fair vs. responsible)
- Part-time psychologist
- Character

Delegation

- Why? Time management and training
- To be able to discern when, when not to, and how?

Potential Problem Areas

- Partying
- Not meeting goals
- Personal interface
- Entrepreneurship vs. team success
- Too high achievers
- Systems for accountability and responsibility
- Third-party sales reps

Best Attributes of Sales Personnel

- Personable
- Approachable
- Good listener
- Articulate
- Professional appearance
- Speaking and presenting skills
- Writing skills
- Persistent

- Closing skills
- Caretaking skills
- Socializing skills (golf, tennis, fishing, sports, culinary, travel)

Running of Meetings

- Clear agenda and time frame
- Who has to bring what; expectations of attendees
- Start and end on time
- Keep bullshit to a minimum
- Reduce effect of personalities
- Make it interesting
- Bring closure
- Bring something new and innovative to each session
- Keep face to face, when possible
- Conference calling?

Prospecting and Lead Generation

Interviewing

- Legal issues
- Ask questions; listen and give time for answers
- Be direct
- Outline examples and ask how they would handle
- What would we like best and what would need improvement
- Tests?
- Always have someone else interview
- Call referrals; also an account they lost
- Profile resume: length of job, where, positions, salary history, reason for leaving; look for patterns, excuses, etc.
- Watch their demeanor, expressions, eye contact
- Identify necessary skill sets for the position; ask them to discuss how they are with each; get details

Negotiation Best Practices Outline: 10 Steps

Thomas A. Cook

1. Go to school
2. Master this skill set
3. Study the psychology of need and people's behavior
4. Compromise
5. Create the win-win scenario
6. Mine heavily
7. Articulation is key
8. Sell to the decision makers
9. Control the venue
10. Make it so it sells itself

Go to School

Negotiation is an important skill set for sales personnel and, in actuality, for all management staff. It allows for success to have the best opportunity. How is it indoctrinated into the salesperson? Some of that will come from senior and colleague mentoring. Some negotiation skills are innate. Some are achieved over time. But the faster we learn these skills, the faster success will follow. You need to take formal classes in negotiation skill sets.

The following schools offer excellent training classes:

American Management Association: www.amanet.org
The World Academy: www.theworldacademy.com
Karrass: www.bothwin.com

The World Academy has one-on-one training with in-house classes available. Karrass (bothwin.com) has an excellent reputation and teaches all over the country on a regular basis. The American Management Association (AMA) is a leading corporate trainer and offers lots of sales management and negotiation classes.

Negotiation skill set training is a work-in-process, meaning it should be continually occurring and being kept contemporary.

Master This Skill Set

Never get arrogant about this. You may be a good negotiator, but you can always get better.

As a sales manager, if you are going to be of value to your sales staff and be a leader, then you need to master this negotiation skill set. There is no option here, as this skill set gets orders and helps maintaining clients and making new business development a hell of a lot easier.

There are advanced classes given and programs that can be easily modified for individual needs. The World Academy (www.theworldacademy.com) is an excellent option in this regard.

Study the Psychology of Need and People's Behavior

Successful negotiators know human behavior well. They could probably write books about people and how they behave.

It is behavior and character that tell us who we are, how we act, and more importantly, what makes us make the decisions we make. The successful negotiator must have a solid understanding of the following human characteristics:

- How people make decisions
- How people receive information
- How people learn
- What stimuli produce certain results
- How different people react in different sets of circumstances
- Basic people's wants, desires, hopes, and dreams
- Business versus personal decision-making issues

The negotiator, the salesperson, who understands the rudimentary basics of all the items in the previous list will greatly maximize his or her chances of favorable outcomes. This happens because he or she is developing strategy and tactical plans with above-average information flow. This provides a serious and overwhelming advantage.

If you were going into battle and you were offered the choice of three handguns and two grenades or the choice of three handguns, two grenades, two bazookas, and four assault rifles, which would you take? That is how much advantage a negotiator has over someone who does not understand the psychology of how people respond.

Compromise

The willingness to find a midpoint of mutuality where both sides give a little to reach an agreement.

Create the Win-Win Scenario

Negotiate where both sides win rather then one side wins, the other loses. This will allow for a better and more respected result when both sides feel as they have gained.

Mine Heavily

Information is the key to negotiating smart, intelligently and creating the best opportunity for success. Turn lots of stones over to gain insight, knowledge and specific data that can be utilized to gain advantage.

Articulation Is Key

How you say something will directly relate to achieving the desired results. Substance of statement is critical but how it is spoken, delivered and projected can be the link to negotiation success.

Sell to the Decision Makers

The author has observed in over 30 years of negotiation process … failure, not in the approach, but who was approached.

Control the Venue

Negotiate in a neutral settting which might lessen the psychological advantage gained by your opponent. This means that his office might be the wrong place. A conference room might work better or some other location, outside the office.

The setting might have a lot of influence on achieving desired results.

Make It So It Sells Itself

Your pitch and approach should work so you do not have to even ask for the order. Your closing statement and ending dialogue should bring the other party to a favorable conclusion without much need to beg, borrow or grovel.

Your finishing lines should create the atmosphere for a favorable outcome by its own essence. This makes the final job much easier.

Closing Questions

Here are a few questions one could ask to help probe and mine as to where a client prospect's mindset is in respect to your offer and negotiation. Without being overly aggressive or demanding, you could pose the following questions:

Is our presentation and deliverables what you were looking for?
Does our proposal meet your specification?
How do we compare to your other options?
What did you like best about our offer?

Do we fall short in any area?

Do we have any disappointments?

Does this proposal and presentation warrant your consideration for us to obtain the business?

How do we stack up to the competition?

Did we leave anything out that is important to you?

Did we cover everything you anticipated or need to be reviewed?

What can we do or offer to make this deal the most attractive to you?

Sales Management Case Studies Workshop

It is important for sales managers to review and study case studies of likely situations that they might be confronted with, and then proactively come up with various options and solutions to resolve the situation.

The following studies can be utilized in a workshop setting with other sales managers or peers or even sales personnel who have interest in moving ahead.

Some sales managers utilize these case studies with potential sales managers to see how they would respond in a particular situation.

Basic Case Studies

Case 1

You are the newly appointed sales manager. In obtaining this job you left a number of peers and friends behind, who you now have to supervise. The atmosphere is uncomfortable. How do you handle?

Case 2

Two persons were up for the sales management position—you and a good friend. You got the position. Now the relationship is strained, and he will be told that he will be reporting into you. How do you handle?

Case 3

You have been given the job as the sales manager after being one of the top producers for the last three years. But you have never managed before. You are worried and paranoid about what will happen now. What do you do?

Case 4

Sales have been declining for over 18 months. The sales manager has been let go and you have inherited the position. You have several direct sales reports, which are just holding their own. Your charge is to increase sales quickly and significantly. What do you do?

Case 5

You are the newly appointed sales manager. You report to an individual who is a seasoned employee at your firm, but is a technical type, not really sales oriented. You are having difficulty working with him on various sales initiatives and strategies that you want to develop, particularly those with costs attached. How do you handle?

Case 6

You have been in the new sales management position for 6 months. Everything is going pretty well. But you have one woman salesperson who is lagging in sales. She is a single parent and time commitment seems to be a potential issue. How do you favorably resolve?

Case 7

You have six salespersons on site, three off site. The six on site are ahead of sales goals. Two of the other three are way behind, and the other is marginal. What steps can you take to determine what the reasons are and establish rectification?

Case 8

You have been the sales manager for 9 months. Things are not going well. You lost one of the key sales representatives to a competitor, and your numbers are starting to drop. How do you right the ship?

Case 9

You are a younger manager in the organization. With your new sales management responsibilities, you have to interface with older, more seasoned comanagers. You are struggling with the interface, and you are beginning to doubt if they are taking you seriously. You seem to be at the bottom of the totem pole and are beginning to worry if you will be successful in your new position. How do you assess, and what can you do?

Case 10

As a salesperson, you had a lot of control over your time. Now, as a manager, you are putting in 12–14-hour days and working weekends. The pressures and anxieties are mounting. Sales are slipping, and you are feeling a sense of losing control. What do you do?

Case 11

You have 10 sales associates. They are very competitive and very independent. There are a lot of petty issues between them, and shared projects and initiatives are not doing well. There have actually been some minor confrontations, and the atmosphere is difficult and not a good working environment. How do you turn things around?

Case 12

Your business is growing very rapidly. Senior management is putting pressure on hiring new sales representatives. You are struggling to meet this demand. Your area has low unemployment, and the people who are responding to ads are not qualified. How best to handle and make some new hires?

Case 13

You have sales meetings on a regular basis with eight sales associates. Your lead male salesperson is always disruptive, a know-it-all and making what you want to say and accomplish very difficult. He is confrontational, selfish, and a little bit of a bully. He intimidates a lot of people. You are concerned to say something and possibly get him upset and potentially lose him. What are your options?

Case 14

One of your responsibilities in sales management is to coordinate sales orders with manufacturing and shipping. You are new to the sales management position and are beginning to struggle with all sorts of customer complaints, late orders, shipping problems, etc. Senior management is patient with you, but you are beginning to feel the pressure of all the problems. How best to handle and rectify?

Case 15

You have a very successful salesperson whose sales the last year have declined significantly. She has had almost record sales for the 5 previous years. It is beginning to affect company sales overall, and nobody is happy about this dilemma. After being patient, you now have to address the problem, and swiftly. What steps do you take?

Advanced Case Studies

Case I

The company sells IT services to health care companies and has been in business for 17 years, with sales just over $250 million. The company is privately held. Sales have been sliding in most product lines for 9 months and in some of the lead products for the last 3–4 months. Your sales force is relatively seasoned, with a total of nine persons who have over 8 years experience and three persons with only 1–2 years. News from the marketplace advises that many of your competitors are doing much better.

What steps do you take to resolve the dilemma and bring a strategic and tactical response?

Case II

The company manufactures commercial and household generators. It is 60 years old and is publicly traded, with $900 million in sales. The company is considered the leader within the industry over the last 10 years.

You have an aging sales force of over sixteen men and two women. Sales are flat, and while the existing client base is pretty solid, there has been no credible growth into existing markets, and certainly no new markets have opened up. Most of these players are much older than you.

Senior management in the 2008/2009 Business Plan is showing growth of over 15% per annum. They have expressed concern over the existing team's capability to meet the new business goals and have hinted about your ability to lead them there.

They want an outline of a draft strategy by the end of the month. What do you prepare? How do you handle? What do you give them?

Case III

The company is a leader in its market of cosmetics and health care–related products. It is privately held with over $1 billion in sales. You are heading up the sales team, which has thirty health care professionals who are selling direct to high-end clinics, doctor offices, laboratories, and health care facilities.

The sale is highly competitive. The products are expensive. From point of contact to final sale could take as long as 1 year. You have former health care professionals, nurses, and doctor assistants as your sales team. You have two problems: You are losing staff, who lose interest because of the long turnaround time to "close," and you are having a problem recruiting new sales talent.

Provide solutions to both of the problems.

Case IV

The company imports raw materials and components sold to end users. Your customers are major chemical, food, and pharmaceutical companies. You are the U.S. subsidiary of a German company, the North American distributor.

Your product sells well, and you have a few proprietary patents and product lines where the sales are going through the roof. Having said that, your sales team is complaining that the customers are not happy. There are delays in meeting delivery schedules, and some product is coming in with loss or damage. As a result, some customers are seeking alternative suppliers, and you have some seasoned sales representatives frustrated and pretty upset.

How do you handle?

Case V

Your company is being forced by competition to utilize technology in its customer relationships for what previously was a person-to-person-driven business. You are concerned that the new technologies will take out the "relationship" side of the business and put you into a world that is mostly controlled by price and not other value-added services.

How do you handle?

Case VI

The 10-year-old company sells advertising space in outdoor-sports-related magazines, events, and related venues. It is a privately held company with a sales force of eight—four seasoned and four new. Sales are $45 million.

You report to the founder and CEO, who had your job previously as New Business Development Officer/Chief Marketing/VP of Sales, etc. He is very strong minded, opinionated, hands-on, and no nonsense. He hates failure and rewards success. You are quickly losing market share in existing venues to larger competitors, mostly on price-driven-related issues. Some of the larger and loyal customers have begun to stray. The CEO wants you to provide a strategy to "plug" the leaking and rebuild the sales initiatives to the point where he once had them. Your sales force is losing commissions and is unhappy and disenchanted.

What do you do?

Case VII

The company manufactures air conditioning equipment. It is a publicly traded, 30-year-old company with $1 billion in sales. Most of the customers and markets are seasoned.

Your company is solid, but does not have state-of-the-art technology, and its senior management group is a little archaic in its mindset. Some of the products are becoming outdated, and the support services are a little thin.

You had a sales force of ten persons in January of 2006, and it has dwindled to six as of September 2007. Your competitors have the talent that you are struggling to replace. You are now seeing a loss in sales, and you are concerned about meeting year-end numbers and the aggressive plan for 2008. Compensation and opportunity seem to be the reason you have lost most of your people. Obtaining new sales personnel has been next to impossible.

You need a new strategy by the end of November.

What International Salesmen and Travelers Need to Know about U.S. Customs (CBP)

Thomas A. Cook

Under U.S. law, Customs and Border Protection (CBP) officers are authorized to examine travelers and their luggage. Under search authority granted by Congress, every person leaving and entering the United States may be searched and questioned about his or her travel. Hand-carry shipments are considered exports and therefore are subject to the U.S. rules on export controls administered by BIS (Bureau of Industry & Security), CBP, and the Department of State. The following checklist should be reviewed by business travelers, salespeople, and their compliance department prior to departing the United States:

1. If traveling with product samples or actual products, make certain to have proper documentation explaining why the goods are being exported, including a description of the goods and whether or not the goods will be reimported into the United States.
2. If traveling with product samples or sample equipment, confirm with the company's export department as to whether a license is required prior to export. If a license is required, the proper documentation must be submitted and completed prior to departure.
3. Determine whether a Shipper's Export Declaration (SED) is required to be filed prior to export. If an SED is required, file the information electronically using the Automated Export System (AES) and carry a copy of the electronic filing on your person.
4. If traveling with a laptop computer, know whether the computer has encryption capability. If the computer does, review the encryption regulations with the company's corporate compliance officer prior to leaving the United States with the computer.

5. CBP enforces intellectual property rights and looks for possible copyright violations. Determine whether the products being carried violate these regulations, and carry the necessary documentation to demonstrate if licensing has been granted.
6. If carrying currency, be aware of the reporting requirements. Most travelers are aware of the rule that states the transfer of funds (including carrying for export) must be reported to the government for amounts of USD$10,000 or greater. There is a second rule, under the Patriot Act, which covers smaller amounts and includes cash, bank checks, and cashier's checks.
7. AES became mandatory in 2005 and is in full force and effect in 2009.
8. Customs has determined from the data collected by AES that exporters are not properly documenting Commerce licenses. At the time of this writing, exporters are responsible for documenting their exports and obtaining their own licenses. However, audit teams have found many companies' records to be shoddy, with violations ranging from gross negligence to criminal levels. Record keeping must be a part of the business travelers' process, as they are carrying the goods and may be held accountable for facilitating the passage of goods from the United States to overseas.
9. CBP has access to electronic passenger lists and reviews these lists prior to departure of outbound flights to pinpoint potential target investigations. In addition, the Transportation Security Administration (TSA) will notify CBP if they feel a passenger is suspicious and requires further examination by authorities.

How is CBP able to fund these changes and enforcement actions? With the restructuring of CBP, including the addition of immigration personnel who have now been combined with CBP, there are a tremendous amount of personnel dedicated to outbound and overall CBP enforcement.

WHY HAVE YOU ACCEPTED THIS POSITION?

■ Money
■ Security
■ Career Opportunity

WHAT ARE YOUR CONCERNS OR FEARS ABOUT THESE NEW RESPONSIBILITIES?

■ Failure
■ Co-workers … what will they think?
■ Hours and time commitment?
■ Leadership skills?
■ Ability to meet goals and execute strategies

WHAT ARE YOUR EXPECTATIONS FROM THIS SEMINAR AND CLASS?

■ Stay out of trouble
■ Make you think
■ Learn options and betterments
■ Share methods and ways
■ Assist in goals, strategies and executions
■ Make it easier for me.

MANAGEMENT VS. LEADERSHIP?

■ Difference
■ Importance in Understanding
■ "Character" Issue

EXECUTION AND CONSISTENCY: SUCCESS OR FAILURE

■ Importance of Understanding
■ Hardest Part of Succeeding in Sales
■ Commitment…Just Do It.

WHEN TO BE A FATHER, MOTHER, SISTER, PREACHER, DISCIPLINARIAN, EDUCATOR, HAND-HOLDER, MENTOR OR FRIEND?

- Determine "hat" to wear
- Approach will determine success
- Sometimes within a conversation or a dialogue...you will wear more than one hat

WHY DO PEOPLE BUY?

- Need or you convinced them so
- PRice
- Service
- Time Frame

*** Character: Honest, Integrity, Being Responsible, Doing what you say, team player, for the good of the company, caring, considerate, unselfish, etc.

Index

About the Author

Thomas Cook has been involved in sales and global business for more than 28 years in an array of diverse international trades.

He graduated from Maritime College at Fort Schuyler, New York, where he earned both a B.S. in transportation science and a graduate degree in transportation and business management. His career began in the U.S. Naval Reserve and in the U.S. and Dutch Merchant Marine, where he served as an officer in various capacities all over the globe. Tom has also been involved in the international insurance, manufacturing, exporting, sales and marketing, and trade finance arenas, in senior management and equity positions, with an emphasis on sales, business development, and management operations.

He has authored over 250 articles and several books on international trade, business and sales, and has lectured worldwide on numerous subjects involved with global trade. Tom is currently an adjunct professor at the World Trade Institute of Pace University in New York, teaching courses on logistics, international sales, and transportation management. He is the seminar leader for the import/export seminars for the American Management Association (AMA) in New York. He also serves on the board of the District Export Council of New York.

Tom leads various programs in sales management at AMA, IOMA, the World Academy and the World Trade Institute. He has developed numerous sales management programs and initiatives in training corporate executives in domestic and international sales. He currently is managing director of American River International, a premier international sales and business management consulting company based in New York City.